CHARITY

Catholic Spirituality for Adults

General Editor
Michael Leach

Other Books in the Series

CHARITY

✳

Virgil Elizondo

Maryknoll, New York 10545

Founded in 1970, Orbis Books endeavors to publish works that enlighten the mind, nourish the spirit, and challenge the conscience. The publishing arm of the Maryknoll Fathers and Brothers, Orbis seeks to explore the global dimensions of the Christian faith and mission, to invite dialogue with diverse cultures and religious traditions, and to serve the cause of reconciliation and peace. The books published reflect the views of their authors and do not represent the official position of the Maryknoll Society. To learn more about Maryknoll and Orbis Books, please visit our website at www.maryknollsociety.org.

Library of Congress Cataloging-in-Publication Data

Elizondo, Virgilio P.
    Charity / Virgil Elizondo.
        p.   cm. – (Catholic spirituality for adults)
    ISBN 978-1-57075-720-4
    1. Church work with Hispanic Americans. 2. Charity. 3. Love – Religious aspects – Catholic Church. I. Title.
    BV4468.2.H57E45 2008
    241′.4 – dc22

                                                            2008020451

To my parents and sister,
Virgilio, Ana Maria, and Anita,
in whom I have experienced
the creative beauty of love

Contents

Introduction to
Catholic Spirituality for Adults

C ATHOLIC SPIRITUALITY FOR ADULTS explores the deepest dimension of spirituality, that place in the soul where faith meets understanding. When we reach that place we begin to see as if for the first time. We are like the blind man in the Gospel who could not believe his eyes: "And now I see!"

Catholicism is about seeing the good of God that is in front of our eyes, within us, and all around us. It is about learning to see Christ Jesus with the eyes of Christ Jesus, the Way, the Truth, and the Life.

Only when we *see* who we are as brothers and sisters of Christ and children of God can we begin to *be* like Jesus and walk in his Way. "As you think in your heart, so you are" (Prov. 23:7).

Catholic Spirituality for Adults is for those of us who want to make real, here and now, the words we once learned in school. It is designed to help us go beyond information to transformation. "When I was a child, I spoke as a child, I understood as a child, I thought as a child, but when I became an adult, I put away childish things" (1 Cor. 13:11).

The contributors to the series are the best Catholic authors writing today. We have asked them to explore the deepest dimension of their own faith and to share with us what they are learning to see. Topics covered range from prayer — "Be still, and know that I am God" (Ps. 46:10) — to our purpose in life — coming to know "that God has given us eternal life, and this life is in his Son" (1 John 5:11) — to simply getting through the day — "Put on compassion, kindness, humility, gentleness, and patience" (Col. 3:12).

Each book in this series reflects Christ's active and loving presence in the world. The authors celebrate our membership in the mystical body of Christ, help us to understand our spiritual unity with the entire family of God, and encourage us to express Christ's mission of love, peace, and reconciliation in our daily lives.

Catholic Spirituality for Adults is the fruit of a publishing partnership between Orbis Books, the publishing arm of the Catholic Foreign Mission Society of America (Maryknoll), and RCL Benziger, a leading provider of religious and family life education for all ages. This series is rooted in vital Catholic traditions and committed to a continuing standard of excellence.

Michael Leach
General Editor

Acknowledgments

I am grateful to the many persons who have helped me to make this book possible — certainly, as you will see, my family, friends, and parishioners from whom I have learned so much. The teams at the Mexican American Cultural Center and CTSA-TV in San Antonio and the Institute for Latino Studies at the University of Notre Dame have been inspiring and supportive. My colleagues and close friends in the theology department of Notre Dame, especially Father Daniel Groody, C.S.C., and Professor Timothy Matovina, were most helpful with their critical comments and suggestions. I am most appreciative of the great wisdom gained through conversations with Father Tim Scully, C.S.C., and Father Richard Warner, C.S.C., of Notre Dame and Father Kevin Kostelnik, rector of the Cathedral of Our Lady of the Angels in Los Angeles, as well as through the many other good conversations with the priests and brothers of the Congregation of the Holy Cross working in Notre Dame.

In a very special way, I am grateful to Father John Jenkins, C.S.C., president of the University of Notre Dame, who asked the entire university to reflect on Benedict XVI's encyclical on charity: *Deus Caritas Est*. The many conversations and work sessions with professors and students from the various faculties, led by Professor Sabine MacCormack, resulted in many good insights that became part of this book.

I would like to thank the many students who over the years have contributed to this work: Pat Dillingham, Brady Quinn, Penny Wolf, Victor Abiamiri, Ambrose Wooden, Rocio Aguinaga, Brett Lilley, Pat Lopez, Evan Sharpley, Brian Sheehan, Susan Pinnick, Adriana Stasuik, and many others.

A very special thanks goes to my archbishop, José H. Gomez, and the priests, deacons, religious, and laity of San Antonio, and in particular the people of my parish of St. Rose of Lima, who have always been supportive and encouraging of my work. Their dedication continues to be a great inspiration.

I am especially grateful for the confidence placed in me by Michael Leach, the editor of this series on Catholic Spirituality for Adults. Without his invitation I would have never worked on this book, as well as for his helpful suggestions. Finally I am grateful to everyone who will read this book and pray that it will be beneficial in their efforts to put on the mind and heart of Christ, who is the incarnation of the love of God.

Author's Introduction:
Truly Successful Lives

What profit would there be for one to gain the whole world and forfeit his life. — Matthew 16:26

CHARITY IS SIMPLY about actively living the ultimate truth about life. It is simply love in action, for love is the very essence of human life; it is what ultimately makes us fully human, fully alive. It is the love that arises out of the recognition that we are all images and likenesses of God — of Love itself; for God is love (1 John 4:17). Thus what we do unto each other we truly do unto ourselves and to God. Charity is allowing the life of God to work through our ordinary, sometimes extraordinary, deeds and words of daily life because God is love! Charity is each one of us, all of us, manifesting God-Love in the world often estranged from God and true expressions of love. In this world plagued by so many distractions and even distortions, nothing could be more fulfilling, beautiful, and inspiring than a life of love in action. It is in love that we reach the fullness of life.

Nowhere is the life of love more truly manifested than in the life and teachings of Jesus, who himself is the incarnation of infinite love. Since the Gospels use life stories to teach about the deepest truths about us humans, about society, and about God, I would like to begin reflecting on charity by telling you a few stories about good friends of mine whose whole life was characterized by a spirit of love and concern for others in need. Two of them were the toughest, most successful professionals I have ever met and at the same time the most charitable persons one could ever imagine. They were charitable beyond measure. The other two were persons that could easily have been great hotel or mega-store managers, but they chose to live a simple life of loving service to others.

The first one was James P. McLaughlin. I first met him while he was president/CEO of United Parcel Service and I was president of the Mexican American Cultural Center in San Antonio. We had been helping to prepare UPS personnel to understand the people and culture of the Southwest of the United States, and UPS had become a great supporter of MACC. On one of his visits to San Antonio, I had the privilege of meeting Jim, and we immediately became good friends.

Very early in life, Jim had lost his father, and his mother had struggled to raise the family of two girls and one boy. Yet she managed not only to give them a good Catholic education but also to be generous with those in greater need. Soon after graduating from school, Jim started working for the newly formed UPS: first as a runner and gradually moving up the ladder of responsibility until he became its president. I am told he could be the toughest administrator and negotiator, yet he never lost concern for the poor and needy. He was always concerned with giving the underprivileged a chance. I don't know if he was the one who instituted the policy, but one of the things that impressed me deeply about him was that when he noticed a young UPS executive who seemed to have a lot of potential for top leadership, he would have the person do a six-month internship in one of the poverty areas of the United States, working with underprivileged children. He felt that if the person did well in working with the poor, that person had the necessary qualities to be a top leader in the company.

Jim became a very wealthy man, yet he never forgot those in need. His love and concern for his family of seven children was evident in many ways, especially in his ability to teach them by example the ways of a loving God, a God who expects us to be generous with others as God is with us. Jim never bought fancy homes, resort properties, yachts, automobiles, jewelry, or the like. His great delight was in finding ways of making life better for others, in finding ways of helping the underprivileged of society find opportunities, in opening the doors for others to enjoy the American dream. Charity was not an obstacle to toughness and success in our competitive society but rather the very source and summit of a truly successful life. James P. McLaughlin was a person who truly embodied and lived out the charity of Christ.

❖

I have been fortunate to encounter many persons like Mother Teresa, persons for whom loving service to others was their ordinary way of life. They were not sad persons, but rather radiated a beautiful peacefulness and often had a healthy laugh and sense of humor. One such person is Janie Dillard, who has been my close associate both at San Fernando Cathedral and at the Mexican American Cultural Center for many years.

Life has never been easy for her, yet she is the hardest working, most generous, and most joyful person I have ever met. When she was eight years old, her parents divorced, and her father abandoned the family. While her mother held two jobs to keep the family going, by the age of eleven Janie was already cleaning homes, doing laundry for neighbors and working at other domestic jobs. When her mother died of cancer, a judge gave her legal custody of their household of three brothers and sisters even though she was only fourteen years of age. It was at that time, having dropped out of school to take care of her family, that she started working at a restaurant. She had learned early in life that you had a choice when bad things happened: let them destroy you through self-pity or allow them to make you stronger, better, and wiser. "I chose the latter," she says. This is the Janie I have come to know and admire.

From these good friends I have learned the important lesson that the sign of truly successful persons — whether rich or poor — is the charitable spirit that animates and directs their lives.

Besides being very active in her parish, for many years she served as the volunteer assistant to Archbishop Flores in reaching out to poor people, helping them with food, utilities, and rent money, arranging for pauper funerals, helping with baby diapers, school clothing, and many other needs. Later on, she moved to San Fernando Cathedral to assist me with the many activities of a downtown church, one of which was welcoming the many street people who came by requesting help. She was always there, treating everyone with respect, dignity, and friendship. Janie was not only deeply involved in helping the poor and doing good for others; she was always conscious of her primary obligation as a wife, mother, and grandmother. She is truly a multi-talented person who could easily have been a great success at any major enterprise, but she chose to live a simple life of loving service to others and in so doing she has found a deep sense of satisfaction and fulfillment.

※

Patrick Maloney was a San Antonio boy who lied about his age in order to enlist in the U.S. Marine Corps to fight in World War II. He saw action in the Pacific front and lost many of his close friends in battle. He was one of the fortunate ones to return alive. Through many struggles, Pat became one of the most successful trial lawyers in the United States and was a close advisor of many political leaders, including presidents of the United States.

When I was a boy, Pat Maloney was a legend in San Antonio because of his involvement in issues of social justice. We became close friends when I was assigned to be rector of San Fernando Cathedral. Pat started every day of his life with early morning meditation and daily Mass at 6:00 a.m. We had great conversations every morning about local and world affairs, and he was always ready to help anyone I would send to him. Pat loved to have people for lunch in the dining room — the "Longhorn Room" — of his downtown office. Anyone was welcomed, and Pat always made visitors feel as if they were the most important people in the world. He took a personal interest in every one of his visitors, asking about their families, their work, even their hobbies.

The only thing that exceeded his brilliance and toughness as a lawyer was his warm and generous heart. He was a man of great compassion whom you could always count on to be involved in good causes. He once told me that he had to become the best lawyer possible because he was defending the "nobodies of society" against the giant corporations. He used the law in the best sense: to defend the powerless against the powerful and to allow the voiceless to have a voice. He was truly a giant. Yet he never forgot his humble origins in the South Side of San Antonio, the foundations of his Catholic faith, and his love for making the American dream possible for everyone.

❖

There is one final story I would like to share, although I have many more that I will leave for another time. Maria Teresa Garza is my associate at the University of Notre Dame. Terry, as she is affectionately known by her friends, has been divorced for a long time. She has one very successful daughter, brothers and sisters, and elderly parents. She is the eldest of a family of twelve. As is the case for many Mexican Americans, her upbringing in a small south Texas town was difficult yet spiritually very rich. She often recalls how her grandmother taught the children to pray and play, how the family worked picking cotton during the hot Texas summers, and how they all enjoyed celebrating the family feasts. When I asked her how she had obtained the marvelous spirit of charity that is the guiding force in her life, she responded immediately: "From the times my parents taught us to be *servicial* — of willing service to others. I might add that in our Latino culture, one of the greatest compliments one can make is to say that a person is very *servicial*. She went on to add: "I just feel good doing good for others."

Terry has been working for the church in the Midwest since 1971. Terry is one of those persons whose spontaneous sense of service with a smile appears to be her very nature. Whether for a student, a maintenance worker, a professor, a bishop, or the president of the university, she is always ready to be of service with the same joyful spirit and loving concern. She is extremely efficient and could easily be manager of a major corporation, yet she has chosen to dedicate her life to helping others through her work at the university and in the church.

From these good friends I have learned the important lesson that the sign of truly successful persons — whether rich or poor — is the charitable spirit that animates and directs their lives. Christian life is not opposed to material success but rather guides it to become a source of ultimate fulfillment, true happiness, and even eternal life.

❖

I was fascinated when the first major teaching to come from the newly elected Pope Benedict XVI was the encyclical on the primacy of charity, that is, the mystery of Christian love. Because he had been the Vatican's doctrinal master charged with safeguarding the orthodoxy of the faith, I suppose everyone expected that his first pronouncement would be on one or another doctrinal issue. Well, precisely because he has such a deep and clear appreciation of Christian doctrine, he went to the basis of all Christian doctrine: love. Without love, the whole edifice of Christian teaching and worship is drained of its ultimate life-source. Without love, Christian morality becomes a destructive system of rules and regulations rather than the joyful living of a new life of generosity. Without love, religious people quickly become hateful hypocrites. Without love, our Christian churches become lifeless monuments rather than places of encounter with the God who is love.

Charity is the life of loving others out of the deepest desires of our heart. It is a gift of God. We can love because we have experienced the love of God. God loved us first! (1 John 4:10). Charity is not just a spontaneous and casual good deed but a lifetime of joyfully sharing with others what we are and what we have, not because we have to but because we want to. It is the spontaneous and most natural result of living in communion with God, who is love itself. Love is that intense inner desire for togetherness, participation, and communion with the object of my desire, and charity is the living out of this love as we strive to make life better for those whom we love. Ultimately it is about the gift of self for the sake of others. It is the natural law of a loving heart and not a law imposed by external regulations and demands. It is a desire and not an imposition. Even though it might be very demanding and time-consuming, it is never an odious burden. Even when it demands sacrifice and abnegation, it is still joyful and deeply satisfying, for it is in giving and sharing that we reach the fullness of our being.

The great tragedy is that the notion of love has remained so underdeveloped in many and so confused and even perverted in others. Modern society has advanced in many ways, but has it advanced in its ability to love? It even seems that the more we develop technologically and advance in material comforts, the more we lose the ability to love. Our modern day is not conducive to loving relationships because competitive society makes us rivals of each other rather than partners.

Even working husbands and wives easily become rivals rather than partners.

It is in and through Jesus, through every detail of his life, works, and words, that the very nature of love is purified and clarified. It is this unselfish life of total dedication and loving service to others that we have come to know as charity. Jesus himself is charity personified, and only in him does the true nature of love as the ultimate fulfillment of the deepest desires of the human heart become visible and tangible. In Jesus, infinite and unconditional love became a flesh-and-blood human being, becoming just one of the masses of humanity, yet loving us like no one else had ever loved. As Teilhard de Chardin would say, in Jesus a whole new species of humanity erupts, a humanity that is not only capable of infinite possibilities of thought, but one that now has infinite possibilities of love. Jesus is not only the revelation of true and authentic charity; through our encounter with him, we become capable of loving others as he has loved us.

We experience this infinite love of God when we come into personal contact with the deeds and words of Jesus as his followers live them today. No teaching or doctrine is more powerful, more beautiful, or more convincing than the witness of truly charitable persons. Charity, as we will try to show in these essays, is expressed in diverse ways and various degrees. Some live it out in the simple yet heroic struggles of daily life, for example, parents who work hard to provide for their children, a social worker who works with the poor, or a dedicated teacher. Others, like Damien the leper priest, Cesar Chavez, Dorothy Day, and Martin Luther King lived it out in a more extraordinary and visible way. Still others, who sacrifice their lives trying to cross the border into the United

States to seek sustenance for their starving families, live it out as invisible victims of the unjust structures of our society.

> Nothing is more practical than finding God, that is, than falling in love in a quite absolute, final way. What you are in love with, what seizes your imagination, will affect everything. It will decide what will get you out of bed in the morning, what you do with your evenings, how you spend your weekends, what you read, who you know, what breaks your heart, and what amazes you with joy and gratitude. Fall in love, stay in love and it will decide everything.   —Pedro Arrupe, S.J., 1981

——————————————————

Chapter One

A School of Charity

As I have loved you, so you also should love one another.
— John 13:35

SINCE THE EARLIEST days of my life I have known about charity. I never studied about charity or read books about it; I simply lived it. I certainly did not know the word, except that it was the name of one of the girls at school, but I experienced the reality in my daily life. For my parents and entire family, charity was simply the ordinary way of life and the primary consideration in all things. Respect and concern for others was my family's way of life. We never thought it could be otherwise. In my home, the measure of a good education was not how much schooling you had had or how many degrees you had obtained, or what schools you had attended. A well-educated person was one who was always respectful of others and concerned about their welfare. The product of a good education was the formation of a loving heart, a heart willing to sacrifice for the sake of others.

My parents had both immigrated from Mexico during very difficult times and at a very young age. My mother had come from Mexico City as a young teenager with her mother, who had been widowed and had lost everything. My dad had come from a very small town in northern Mexico at the age of thirteen, not knowing any English and seeking to find work so that he could send money back to his starving family in Mexico. My mother learned a bit of English and also learned how to type. She was able to find a secretarial job with a patient lawyer who helped her with the many English words she didn't know. She used to walk several miles to work every day because she could not afford the money for the bus. My dad found an uncle who had always lived in San Antonio and got a job in my uncle's grocery store, but he had to sleep in an outdoor shed because there was no room for him in the small family home. Eventually my parents met, married, and started a new life together. They were survivors, and no amount of difficulty was to diminish their hope for a better life.

Life had never been easy for them in Mexico or the United States, but like many of the poor, struggling immigrants I have met, they never doubted the goodness of God. They truly lived in God's presence. In spite of the many hardships, setbacks, and even racist insults they had endured, I never heard them complain. On the contrary, they never ceased thanking God for what they had and for the privilege of living in the United States. We were not a rich family materially, but we were very wealthy spiritually. My parents were not very churchy people, but they had a deep sense of and appreciation for the loving presence of God in our lives. I don't think they ever read the Bible or studied the catechism, but I have no doubt that they knew God quite well and were on intimate terms with God. My father even loved telling God the best jokes he had heard each day. He used to say: "If God is truly God, he must enjoy a good laugh." I love this image of a laughing God, a God enjoying life and inviting us to enjoy life with him and each other. Sometimes I wonder why we always seem to portray God as a stern and even mean fatherly figure. Yet laughter is a great gift of God that allows us to rise above the tensions and trials of life in the realization that there are always greater things to come. A good sense of humor allows us to relativize many of the things that we tend to be overly concerned about. Maybe this sense of a loving-laughing God was the source of my dad's laughter. In spite of the many struggles and difficulties, my dad always appreciated humor and had a very healthy laugh.

Even as my father was dying of cancer back in the days when they did not have the care and the painkillers they have today, he never stopped thanking God for God's goodness and generosity. In late October 1964, a few days before his death, he had been in tremendous pain throughout the day. All of a sudden, around nine in the evening he noticed some Halloween decorations in the room and asked what day it was. When we told him, he became very sad because he was keeping the nurses and hospital workers from trick or treating with their children. He asked us to call the family store and get all the candy available and bring it to him right away so that in some small way he could make up for their loss of fun with their children. When the candy arrived, he asked for the hospital personnel to come to the room and he started to pass out the bags of candy. His great generosity in forgetting himself for the sake of others had transformed the pain into ultimate bliss. What the drugs had not been able to accomplish his generosity had been able to bring about. During those brief moments, it seemed like all the pain was gone and his face radiated joy and tranquility. Because of this spirit of loving gratitude, my parents were the most charitable and happiest people I have ever met.

Mom and dad owned a small family grocery store where working to make ends meet was a daily struggle. (A painting of our family store, by artist Jesse Trevino, can be seen at the Smithsonian Institution in Washington, D.C., under the title *Tienda de Elizondo*.) They had opened the store during the Depression with money my mother had saved by buying her wedding dress from an outlet rather than from a fancy store. My dad used to say that if he had stayed in Mexico he would have been someone's peon, but here he was his own boss. He loved the fact that by developing his own business he did not work for anyone. This in fact meant working all the harder, because if he didn't work well and responsibly, the business would fail. For my dad, creating and developing his own business was one of the great blessings of the freedom and equality that were possible in this country. We all worked at the store, often getting up to go to the farmers market at three in the morning to be able to get the best vegetables fresh from the farms. From early morning to late at night, there was always something to do, whether packing groceries, cutting meat (I became a good butcher and even have a few scars left where I sliced my fingers), unloading hundred-pound sacks of flour, sugar, or beans, waiting on customers or simply visiting with whoever would come in. In many ways, our store functioned as a community center, where family news and gossip were easily exchanged.

In spite of their many struggles just to keep the store going, my parents enjoyed helping those in need. Dad would help materially and my mother with good advice — she functioned as the community counselor. No one who asked for help was sent away empty-handed. Often people would come to the store without money. But they still went home with the

groceries they needed, simply writing the amount due on a slip
of paper. There were no credit cards in those days nor were
there interest charges on late payments. People paid when
they could and, of course, sometimes never. That sure does
not sound like a way to run a successful business, but somehow or another, we stayed in business, paid for our home,
provided for our workers, and ensured that my sister and I
had a good Catholic education. And even years after my dad's
death, my mother would occasionally receive small amounts
of money in payment for what was owed my dad.

Working and sacrificing for the sake of others was not a
burden but a source of joy and laughter. My father's friends
used to tell him that he would soon go broke because he was
giving away so much, but my dad just kept on being generous.
As the Christmas season approached, we would spend hours
wrapping Christmas presents so that everyone who came to
the store would leave with a Christmas present. My dad used
to say that you could never outdo God in generosity and, sure
enough, the more he gave, the more opportunities seemed to
open up. But the greatest blessing was to end the day knowing
that you had made life a bit better, a bit easier, a bit hap-
pier for others. My dad used to say that this was the greatest
wealth in the world. He had had very little schooling, yet he
knew more about the mystery of life than any scholar I have
ever met.

My dad ran the store, but my mom was the neighborhood
counselor. It is amazing to me today how often I run into
very successful persons who tell me that it was thanks to my
mother's encouragement and advice that they decided to stay
in school and go to college. In the days I was growing up in

San Antonio, many of our public schools discouraged Mexican American youth from advancing in education. They often convinced our children that they were not good enough to even think about the professions. My mother countered this by constantly bringing out the good and challenging them to believe in themselves and go for the top. I have come to learn that this is a profound aspect of charity: not just helping people in material need, but also helping the needy to believe in themselves, to appreciate their dignity, to value their infinite worth, and to dare to achieve what society and its teachers tell them they are incapable of obtaining. Mom was a master at this. This is the deepest root of my preaching and teaching today, for it really pains me to see how many people do not believe in themselves or value their talents and abilities and hence waste their lives away feeling sorry for themselves. At my mother's funeral a childhood friend came up to my sister and me and said: "Memi [as her friends used to call her] was our Mother Teresa."

My parents knew that just helping others in need was not enough. We had to help change the society that made life miserable for our people and excluded us from many of the structures of opportunity. My parents and most of the people in our neighborhood became citizens so that they could vote and take part in the decision-making process. This was a great country but far from perfect, and the exciting thing was that we could take a part in making it better. I remember the great enthusiasm as I went with my dad to meetings of associations for the betterment of our people. Even if it was difficult, we had to work to break down the walls of exclusion that kept so many people in misery. From my earliest days, I remember our involvement in civic and cultural causes. I remember selling bingo tickets to help elect Henry Gonzalez as our first Mexican American city councilman. He eventually became our first U.S. congressman and one of the most respected members of Congress. Today, his son Charlie Gonzalez has succeeded him at this post. We worked hard to help repeal the poll tax that had been designed to keep poor blacks and Mexican Americans from voting. Civic involvement was collective charity in action. Today this same spirit continues through the efforts of community organizing groups that work for better human conditions for entire neighborhoods.

My parents knew that just helping others in need was not enough. We had to help change the society that made life miserable for our people and excluded us from many of the structures of opportunity.

We organized local Mexican American merchants to establish our own bank so that we could have a voice in the management of our money. My mom would always dress up with great pride to attend the annual shareholders meeting of the bank. My parents used to say that rather than wasting our time complaining we should devote our energies to creating new structures of opportunity. Complaining makes us bitter and sucks the life out of the soul while creative struggles fill us with life and positive energy.

Merchants organized to help one another. Healthy business was not about competition but about collaboration. The best way for business to prosper was to help others prosper along with you; there will always be enough for everyone. I remember them saying that the best way of helping people is to make life better for everyone. Thus even in business concern for others was the underlying spirit. This attitude was totally different from today's spirit of uncontrolled avarice that drives the big national chains to drive the small local businesses out of existence. Even in good business, charity can be a guiding principle. Avarice will end up destroying everyone while charity can lead to lasting success for everyone.

But it wasn't just the political and social issues that were important. We were also very involved in celebrating and promoting the best of our Mexican heritage. We started our own Spanish-language radio station and soon after television came to life, we started the first Spanish-language TV station in the United States, which later became UNIVISION. We celebrated the *fiestas patrias* on September 16 (Mexican Independence Day) with our traditional Mexican dances, music, and decorations, often bringing in the best Mexican movie stars to celebrate with us. We might well be away from Mexico but Mexico was not away from us. It was in our hearts and souls, and nothing expressed this better than our traditional songs and dances. I can well remember the huge crowds filling the municipal auditorium with songs of *Viva México, Viva América, tierra bendita de Dios.*

The feast of Our Lady of Guadalupe with the predawn celebrations was the great affirmation of the new life that she continued to bring about. In the early morning chill of December we experienced the warmth of being together as a united people, almost as if we were one body, one soul, and one heart. There were always plenty of flowers, dancers, singers, prayers, dramatizations, and, of course, good tamales y chocolate — the ancient food of the gods! The other great religious events that brought us together were the annual celebrations of Holy Week with the rich and colorful pageantry of Palm Sunday, Holy Thursday, and Good Friday. If Guadalupe was the celebration of new life, Holy Week was the celebration of the ultimate gift of God's love for us: Jesus who was willing to sacrifice his life on the cross for our salvation. In the suffering of Jesus our own suffering and struggles took on new life and meaning. We are not alone in our suffering because God continues to be with us. Good Friday was the supreme affirmation of life, of the triumph of ultimate love. Today I see more and more the beautiful depth and transforming power of these beautiful traditions that have enabled suffering peoples to be transformed into joyful survivors and creators of new life.

It is amazing how the cultural celebrations of the impoverished and excluded minority have now become one of the main attractions of our city of San Antonio and in many ways one of the chief economic bases. People love to visit San Antonio because they experience the best of Mexico in the United States. Had we given up and let go of our beautiful foods and traditions, San Antonio would not be the great convention center it has become today. By helping our own people to recognize, affirm, and transmit the great treasures of our heritage, we were enriching the entire city of San Antonio.

As you can see, our love and concern for others was not just personal but equally political, social, cultural, and religious. How could we expect others to respect us and treat us with dignity if we did not appreciate ourselves? How could we love others if we did not love ourselves? How could we have something of value to bring to the country that received us if we threw away the most beautiful treasures of our heritage? There is nothing more destructive and devastating than a deep, often subconscious, self-hatred because of the shame of who we are — a shame in the color of our skin, our body, our name, our foods, our language, our customs, and even our religion. What kept our people alive and well, in spite of the many insults of the dominant society, was the deep, dynamic, and grateful pride because of who we are as a people — children of Our Lady of Guadalupe, the queen of heaven and earth, and descendants of the great civilizations of Spain and ancient Mexico. Who could harm us if we had enjoyed the love and protection of Mary of Guadalupe, the mother of God and our own mother? She had told us, "You have nothing to fear. Am I not here who am your mother?" Her protective and affirming presence has been an incredible life-giving force and a source of great joy and serenity.

Our Catholic faith with its beautiful traditions celebrated through our cultural fiestas was the very ground of our existence, force of our survival, and the source of our joy. We knew that society had to change to make things better for everyone, but this change would begin within ourselves and our communities. We didn't know the words but our hearts knew that action on behalf of justice was an essential constituent of charity. And justice was not just about civil rights and living wages. Yes, it was this and much more. It is about helping people who have been broken and injured by society become whole by regaining confidence in themselves and their culture; it is about incorporating the excluded into society; it is about recognizing and valuing the talents of every person and culture. The joyful celebration of our cultural and religious traditions was truly an act of communitarian charity, for in the very celebrations there was a spontaneous acceptance, affirmation, and uplifting of everyone without exception. I don't suppose people ordinarily see fiesta as charity, but a fiesta wherein everyone is welcomed is truly the embodiment of charity itself, for love transcends commonly divisive barriers. And this is what happens in fiesta.

This spirit of joyful, sacrificing love was most evident in our home. The love my parents had for each other was manifested in the way they cared for each other, always putting the needs of the other ahead of their own. As I think back, I remember how each seemed intent on bringing out the good qualities of the other and loved to speak about them to others. They both loved to brag about each other to friends and family. Many years after my dad had died, and even up until the moment she died, my mom kept talking about the great and generous man my dad had been. Their love allowed them to see good qualities and talents others might have ignored, for that is the nature of true love: to penetrate the deepest recesses of the personality of the beloved and to see beauty and value that others might not see.

My mom and dad were very different in many ways and I am sure that there must have been disagreements between them, yet I never recall seeing or hearing them argue or get into a fight. They would patiently discuss matters, truly listen to one another, and gradually come to agreement. As kids, we used to try to put one against the other to get what we wanted, but it never worked, for they always seemed to have a way of silent communication that went beyond our childish attempts at manipulation.

The greatest inheritance my parents left us is the memory of how they loved one another, how they loved us, and how this love extended to anyone we came in contact with. Charity was not an abstract teaching but the heart and soul of our everyday life. My parents had little, but they gave a lot. They had discovered the secret revealed to us through Jesus: God is love, and we are of God when we love one another. Only in love do we come to fulfillment and only in God who is love does our restless heart come to rest. Only in living a life of loving service to others does our heart find ultimate tranquility, peace, and joy.

> I grew up in a wonderful family. I have a lot to be thankful for. And the greatest gift my parents gave me was love.
>
> And of all the lessons my parents taught me, the most powerful one was unspoken, the way they loved one another. My parents taught me the real values in life aren't material, but spiritual. They include faith and family, duty and honor, and trying to make the world a better place.   — Al Gore, 1970

Chapter Two _____

Love Begets Love

Beloved, let us love one another, because love is of God;
everyone who loves is begotten by God and knows God.
Whoever is without love does not know God, for God
is love.   — 1 John 4:7–8

W E BECOME WHO we are through what we experience,
learn, and admire. If I admire a strong gangster, that
is probably what I will aspire to be. Yet this can also work
in a totally different way. If I detest working in the cotton
fields, I'd probably want to find another occupation. A good
friend of mine became a priest, and he has been a very good
one for many years, because he didn't like working on a farm.
Sometimes it is easier to know what I do not want to be than
to discern what I would like to become.

Role models are very important in the formation of life's
goals and aspirations. One of the great defects of today's
religious education programs and theological studies is that
they tend to leave out the lives of our Christian role models,
of those who have lived happily their lives of heroic virtue.
Heroic virtue is not the exclusive domain of the virgins, martyrs, and confessors as we sometimes are led to believe. Heroic
virtue, that is, sanctity, is lived out every day by many ordinary people living very ordinary lives in a heroic way allowing

loving service and dedication to be the guiding principle of their lives. It is these persons who in their very lives reveal the face and heart of a loving God; in and through them we experience the touch of God in our lives. You might say that such persons tenderly massage the love of God through our skins as it gradually reaches our soul and helps in the formation of our personality. It's amazing how many times the loving physical touch of Jesus brought about miraculous healing, and it is this simple touch of love and concern that continues to bring about miracles in the lives of people today.

Unfortunately we have left the creation of role models to secular society, which often exalts and glorifies hedonistic values and lifestyles. It is often the violent who appear as the saints of society, and it is only through violence that earthly salvation seems possible. Just look at any popular movie, electronic game or television program and you will see the triumph of bloody and brutal violence. It seems that violence is the natural law of survival.

Criminal actions make the news, but charitable actions often go unnoticed. I suspect we should be happy that criminal acts make the news; it would be sad if good deeds were so rare that a good deed would be news. But it is still sad to see how much of our country is infested with various types of criminal activity — from stuffing newborn babies into trash cans to blowing up buildings. The great disasters of 9/11 pale in comparison to the number of killings that go on in our country; the worst terrorists are not foreigners sneaking in, but people within our families, churches, and society.

Beyond all the ugly and depressing news about crime and violence, what gives us hope is the lives of the truly charitable persons who make an impact in our lives. In my parish, on the feast of All Saints, I invite the people to reflect with gratitude on the lives of those persons who have been saints to them, those who have touched their lives and made them better persons. When people reflect on this, it is truly beautiful and inspiring to hear the many beautiful examples that come to mind. It might be the criminals who make the news, but we should never lose sight of the many saints that we have living among us, struggling with the many burdens of life yet enriching our lives and the lives of the entire community.

Charity is love in action. It is action on behalf of others arising spontaneously out of a loving heart, a heart that has experienced love and in a very special way has experienced the love of God who is unconditional and unlimited love. These acts of benevolence are not looking for recognition or reward; they simply and very naturally flow out of the generosity of a loving heart. Nobody has to mandate them because they flow out of the deepest desires of a loving person. An excellent summary of love in action is found in the corporal works of mercy: to feed the hungry, to give drink to the thirsty, to clothe the naked, to visit the imprisoned, to shelter the homeless, to welcome the immigrant — especially the immigrant poor — to visit the sick, to bury the dead. These are the very activities, mentioned by Jesus in the Gospel according to St. Matthew (chapter 25), that will be the criteria for our final judgment. Jesus told us this not to scare us into doing good things, but rather to make us aware that it is in living out these activities that we discover the true meaning and purpose of human life. This is the way of life that leads to true fulfillment and integral well-being.

I am sure you have known many truly charitable people, but I would like to tell you about one for whom charity was always his most spontaneous response. The entire life of Archbishop Patrick Flores was one of constant charitable actions. I have many stories to tell about this charitable giant, but I will simply tell you about two incidents that exemplify the spontaneous and extraordinary charitable spirit of this man. One Saturday afternoon I dropped by his apartment for a visit. As I entered his room, he was paging through the telephone directory. I asked him who he was looking for. His response was that he had just heard in the news that a family's home had burned down, and he was looking for their address so that he could drive out to see them and offer them help. Most of us would have assumed that their family and neighbors would be there to help them, but Patrick Flores did not even stop to think who might help them, he simply said: "I am going to help them."

One of the great manifestations of love is the ability to forgive not because we were not hurt, but because love is greater than any human offense.

Another time a man broke into the chancery office, captured the archbishop, and held him captive for several hours while threatening to blow up the whole chancery office with a grenade. The chancery office was quickly evacuated and the entire city went into shock as police officers, FBI agents, law enforcement personnel, police cars, and even fire trucks surrounded the building while helicopters flew low over the area.

The event quickly became a lead item in national and international newscasts. Friends from Europe and Latin America called to ask what was happening. Crowds of concerned people, young and old, surrounded the area and some were holding prayer vigils. Every minute that went by seemed like an eternity as tension and fear mounted.

Finally, around six in the afternoon, the man surrendered. The archbishop refused to press charges, but the state did. At the trial, the archbishop was called upon to testify by the prosecutor, but on the stand Patrick Flores argued in favor of his captor, stating that the man was not a criminal but a mentally sick person who needed help. He argued that the man should not be sent to jail but to a place for mental rehabilitation. The man was nevertheless convicted and sent to jail. At that point the archbishop began supporting the man's family, who were now left without financial support. I never heard the archbishop say anything negative about the man, and it was evident that he held no resentment. It made me think of the first word of Jesus from the cross: "Father, forgive them for they know not what they do" (Luke 23:34). One of the great manifestations of love is the ability to forgive not because we were not hurt, but because love is greater than any human offense.

I could give you many other examples from the life of this great man, whose guiding spirit was always the love of people and the desire to be of service to anyone in need. He traveled to Cuba to help in the release of political prisoners, to Eastern Europe and Latin America for relief services. He founded the National Hispanic Scholarship Fund (which today dispenses millions of dollars yearly in scholarships), and many other national and international works of mercy. But beyond all this, he was always there for anyone in need. He didn't ask any questions; he simply reached out with a helping hand and a loving heart. He was truly a living icon of the Good Samaritan. Now, in his retirement, he ministers by mail to people who are imprisoned for they too need to know that there is someone who still cares for them. This is the only way that rehabilitation will be made possible. Throughout his life, the corporal works of mercy have been the stuff of his everyday life.

At the end of his forty days in the desert, Jesus was hungry, and the devil tempted him by suggesting he turn the stones into bread. Jesus responded: "Not by bread alone does man live, but by every word that comes forth from the mouth of God" (Matt. 4:4). To help those with material needs is absolutely necessary, but never enough. In fact if one helps others only materially there is a great danger of dehumanizing them by reducing them to dependent bodies without a spirit. Material dependency easily robs people of their dignity and freedom. So charity has to go beyond simply handing out food and clothing or helping with rent and utility bills. Because people do not live on bread alone, there are also the spiritual works of mercy through which love can be lived out in our daily lives: to motivate the discouraged, to befriend the lonely, to share in the joys and sorrows of others, to understand the misunderstood, to uplift the lowly and downtrodden, to comfort the sorrowful, to instruct the ignorant, to counsel the doubtful, to forgive the erring, to share faith with the unbeliever, and to offer hope to the desperate. These spiritual works of mercy are the natural and spontaneous attitudes of a loving heart.

Through the practice of the spiritual works of mercy, one liberates and heals the oppressed and wounded human spirit so that persons may begin to believe in themselves — that they are capable, that they are dignified, that they are worthy, that they are lovable. The liberation of the spirit comes through the experience of being recognized, accepted, appreciated, and loved. Once the spirit is liberated and healed, there is no limit to what persons can accomplish. During most of my parish experience, I have worked with the poor. I have discovered that one of the greatest tragedies of constant poverty is that many come to believe that they are not good enough and hence do not even try, or even in trying they carry a defeatist attitude. In all my preaching and teaching I constantly bring out that God who truly knows them not only loves them but needs them and calls them by name to help accomplish God's purpose for humanity. I constantly bring out that the great lie of the world is to convince some that they are inferior and unworthy while the great sin of the world is the exploitation of the poor and defenseless for sake of the "good life" of the rich and powerful. Thus conversion is about rejecting the lie of the world and believing in oneself. Because God believes in me how can I not believe in myself? And believing in myself leads me to recognize and appreciate the dignity and value of other persons.

One of the greatest blessings I experienced as rector of San Antonio's San Fernando Cathedral was that of befriending some of the street people who nobody wanted around. In walking with them, sharing a sandwich with them, and listening to their stories, I learned the transforming power of befriending the lowly and lonely of society. I experienced why Jesus had such a great love for them. In befriending them, they were transformed from being "nobodies" to being human beings, known by name and appreciated because they were human. But most of all, they were transforming me, helping me to see beauty and experience greatness in ways I had never suspected.

I remember an older man named Sam. He lived on the street, was very dark skinned with messy hair, had a few teeth missing, and usually a bad body odor from not bathing. He would stop me in the street and ask for a dollar. "I'm not going to lie to you, Father. I want a dollar for a beer. I'm so ugly nobody wants to talk to me. A cold beer helps me feel good." Sometimes I would come up with things without thinking about them. Instead of giving him the dollar, I invited him to go with me to a bar nearby so we could have a beer together. He started to cry. "Father, nobody wants me around. How come you want to hang around with me?" I simply told him, "because you are my friend and I don't want you to drink alone." That was the beginning of many conversations. A Vietnam veteran, he had been on drugs, became a male prostitute to sustain his drug habit, and had been beaten up several times. His family had long ago told him to stay away. One time, in beautiful handwriting, he wrote me one of the most poignant and painful poems I have ever read about the pain of total aloneness and the hunger for mere acceptance and friendship. I am not sure how much I helped him, but he helped me a lot by giving me many valuable insights into the sufferings of street people. He was not ugly. He was simply a human being in need of being acknowledged. One of the greatest acts of charity is befriending the lonely, the lowly, the excluded and the rejected of society.

Love begets love. It is truly experienced in the acts of benevolence that we experience — the way we are cared for, the way people speak to us, the way we are treated. The best time and place to begin experiencing this love is as babies sucking from our mother's breasts. In the loving embrace of her arms, against the warmth of her body, with the nourishing milk from her breasts, while under the eyes of unconditional love and concern, and feeling the strong protective arms of a loving father, the child begins to experience the infinite love of God who is the author of all life. But even when this experience does not take place, a person still learns to love through the various acts of love experienced in the growing-up process. Love is experienced in a childhood friend, a caring teacher, a friendly bus-driver, a wise coach, a kind janitor, a concerned co-worker, a friendly neighbor, a compassionate priest, and many other persons who in some small way treat me as a valued person whose presence they appreciate. We first see and experience the face and heart of God in the loving dedication and sacrifice of our parents and those who in many ways make themselves parents to us by loving us and helping us to experience that we are lovable.

Coaches and artistic mentors are great practitioners of the spiritual works of mercy precisely because arts and sports are very important in the formation of a person's ability to develop teamwork, self-confidence and self-love. Without this strong base, it will always be difficult for a person to love God and others "as you love yourself" — the great commandment of Jesus. In my many years of teaching at various universities, I have been amazed at how many of the students credit a coach or artistic mentor as one of the persons who had the greatest influence in their lives. Good coaches and mentors have the ability to combine love with discipline, correction with challenge, self-confidence with humility, and excitement with adversity. Two of my students who were star Notre Dame football players and helped me work on this book told me that the greatest lesson they had learned from their high school football coach was that the all-important ingredient of a good team was how the players loved one another.

Love is not just about doing things for people. In fact if we try to do too much for people, we might end up crippling them. I remember a young lady who had been crippled by polio. If she would fall, she could not get up by herself. Her parents were always around to help her until a therapist came to help out. He insisted that they not help her get up, even if she cried and screamed. He would get on the ground and show her how to get up, but he would not help her. Finally, after many tears and even ugly words — "Don't you love me? Don't you care for me?" — she started to get up on her own. In time, she even managed to do simple dances. If people had continued helping her by doing things for her, she would have never gotten up, walked, or danced. Even her personality changed with her ability to get up on her own; she was laughing more and complaining less. The Special Olympics have brought about this type of miracle for thousands of persons.

The tragedy is that there are many healthy persons who are crippled in other ways. There are none more crippled than spoiled persons who always expect things to be done for them but never do anything for themselves. One of the greatest manifestations of love is to help people to discover their talents and gain a healthy sense of self-confidence. Love includes challenging people to rise to the best levels of their potential. A good mentor can be very challenging without being threatening or destructive of the person. I have seen the transformation brought about in children and young people through their participation in theater, sports, music, and the arts.

I remember a Christian Brother by the name of Alexis Gonzalez who would organize fantastic high school theater pieces and carefully place students in the role they most needed to see themselves in. He was an eminently successful director, and the only instruction he would give the students was: "Study the role carefully and ask yourself how would such a character live it out." In the very acting they discovered aspects of life they had not suspected. He didn't have to tell them; he simply led them to discover it. Another such person was the choir director at San Fernando Cathedral, Mary Esther Bernal. It was beautiful to see the rapid transformation of the members of her children's choir from being bashful and timid, burdened with many inferiorities, into self-assured and confident children. Many of the children who started in our children's choir have gone on to become effective schoolteachers, musical directors, professionals, and doctors. Through music and song, children who would probably have gone on to be school dropouts have become very successful and happy persons. I am sure that the thousands of persons who dedicate their time to organize church and neighborhood sports, children's choirs, and other such activities have no idea of the great contribution they are making to the formation of self-confident and loving human beings. Through their coaching and mentoring they are telling the youngsters, "I love you because you are lovable."

The ancient Nahuas, who reigned in Mexico before they were destroyed by European colonization, used to say that an artist was a person with a God-possessed heart because through beauty we come into contact with the divine. Borrowing from them, I would say that charity arises spontaneously out of persons whose hearts God has possessed. There is nothing more beautiful than a loving person whose very presence radiates the beautiful love of God. When someone falls in love, the heart is captured by the beloved. They no longer want to do what they want to do, but what the beloved wants to do. This surrender of the heart is not seen as a diminishing of freedom or a loss of dignity but as the source of ultimate communion and fulfillment. Because God has loved us first, and we have experienced this love not in the abstract but in the encounter with others who have loved us as God loves, we become capable of loving as God alone can love. Charity is the life of one whose heart has been divinized by entering into communion with God's divine love.

> As the Father has loved me, so have I loved you; abide in my love.... This is my commandment, that you love one another as I have loved you. (John 15:9, 12)

The Most Effective Teaching

Above all the Gospel must be proclaimed by witness. Take a Christian or a handful of Christians who, in the midst of their own community, show their capacity for understanding and acceptance, their sharing of life and destiny with other people, their solidarity with the efforts of all for whatever is noble and good. Let us suppose that, in addition, they radiate in an altogether simple and unaffected way their faith in values that go beyond current values, and their hope in something that is not seen and that one would not dare to imagine.... Such a witness is already a silent proclamation of the Good News and a very powerful and effective one. Here we have an initial act of evangelization.

— Pope Paul VI, *Evangelii Nuntiandi*, no. 21,
December 8, 1975

_____

Chapter Three

A Portrait of Love

Whoever has seen me, has seen the Father.
— John 14:9

LOVE AND CHARITY — just what are they? The words are often used in many different ways, often confusing and even destroying the very nature of true love. In a humanity that is starving for love yet finds itself in an infinite confusion about the reality of love, can we ever find out what true love really is? That is what the heart of a person most desires, but just what is it? There is so much pain, disappointment, frustration, anger, and even violence because we seek what we think is love and when we obtain what we are longing for, we find that it deceives us because it is not the fulfilling experience of true love. So, just what is love?

Many philosophers, psychologists, sociologists, and educators have tried to define the essence of the human and have certainly offered many fine insights, but Jesus goes beyond all of them in simplicity, depth, and clarity. Jesus came to reveal the truth of God and the truth of the human. The ultimate truth of both God and humans is love in action, a love that goes beyond oneself to give life to others. This life-giving outpouring of love is charity. God is love, and because man and woman are created in the image and likeness of God, to be fully human is to be a loving person as God is love. As the scriptures tell us that God is love, so then man and woman made in the image and likeness of God are love, and without love we will never be fully human. That is why the desire for love is the deepest longing of the human heart.

When Jesus tells us to be perfect as his heavenly father is perfect (Matt. 5:48), he is telling us to be persons who love unconditionally as God is unconditional love. But his perfection is not the static perfection of a perfectly sculpted Greek statue, which as beautiful as it might be remains lifeless. Biblical perfection is dynamic and creative love. This unconditional and spontaneous love is clarified by Jesus himself when he tells us to be compassionate as his heavenly father is compassionate (Luke 6:36). Compassion in the scriptures is that spontaneous biological reaction when from our innermost bowels we are moved to reach out to those in need. In ancient languages, it referred to the mother's womb that spontaneously reacts to protect the life that it carries. This is the very nature of God, and it is in this image and likeness that we have been created. Unfortunately through sin we have failed to live out our innermost nature, but it is to restore us to the true nature of our being that Jesus came to redeem us. "For God so loved the world that he gave his only Son, so that everyone who believes in him might not perish but might have eternal life" (John 3:16). When Jesus speaks of eternal life, he is not speaking just about the hereafter, but of the new life of loving relationships that begins here and now and will come to its fullness in eternity.

God loves us so much that he gave his son to us and even when we were rejecting his son and demanding his death on the cross, God kept loving us and through his son offering us complete forgiveness and rehabilitation. The mystery of God and the mystery of the human is the very mystery of love itself. Love is a creative and dynamic energy that can never be adequately defined. It is that mysterious force, that inner fire that can consume us without destroying us and can be most demanding of us without enslaving or restricting us. It is a driving desire for union with another and ultimately with God. "Love alone is capable of uniting living beings in such a way as to complete and fulfill them, for it alone takes them and joins them by what is deepest in themselves" (Teilhard de Chardin, *The Phenomenon of Man* [Harper Books, 1961], 265).

Jesus never gave us a clear definition or even a critical theology of love; he was not into that kind of language. This is not to say that he didn't reveal the very source and the effects of this mystery, this inner fire, this driving desire, and this dynamic energy we call love.

The source of love lies within the very nature of God as revealed by Jesus. God is love because out of God's goodness God created and gave us the very beautiful and bountiful world and cosmos that we enjoy. God gave us a sacred earth full of creative powers to provide us with rich varieties of plant and animal life that could serve as beauty to behold and delicious nourishment for our bodies (Gen. 3:6). God is love because rather than keeping to himself, God created man and woman in God's own image and likeness and endowed us with a creative intelligence and free will. Out of God's infinite love, God shared his creative powers with men and women. Out of God's love, God took the risk of creating us humans to be co-creators in the buildup (and even possible destruction) of creation (Gen. 2:15). Out of God's protective and caring love, the universe continues in harmonious motion. Yet a fascinating aspect of the mystery of God's love is that while it is always present it is never imposing. One of the great mysteries of human existence is the relation between God's protective love and our free will. No matter how much we try to understand and explain it, it remains beyond us to comprehend.

Thus we begin to see the elements of charity as love in action. Love first of all is creative; it seeks to bring about new life. Love is sharing with others whatever we have — our possessions, our talents, and our time. But even more than that, love is sharing our very being with others, not out of obligation but out of the desire to enter into communion with others. In the garden of Eden God walked with men and women as friends. God took time just to enjoy the company of Adam and Eve. Love is taking time to be with others. Paradise was the beautiful and harmonious relation between God, man and woman, and nature. In the final moments of his earthly life, Jesus calls his disciples friends. In the Constitution on Divine Revelation of Vatican II, the church tells us that God invites us into the intimacy of friendship with him. In the most holy Trinity, we see that God is loving relationships: Father, Son, and Holy Spirit. It is the same relational life that God wanted to share with us so God created us to live in loving relations with others, with nature, and with God. Without them, we will never be complete, we will never be fully human, we will never truly be the image and likeness of God. That is the reason why alone we are poor. We could be the richest person in the world, the most powerful, the most famous superstar, but without truly loving relations, not just ones of convenience, we would still be poor and even miserable.

Love is also caring for the well-being of creation and those around me. Love is being present to others while never being demanding or imposing, for love always respects the freedom of the beloved. Love is trusting others even when we cannot understand them. Love is faithful and honest companionship. Love is allowing others the space to grow and develop into their own proper self without trying to make them clones of ourselves. This is another of the great mysteries of God's love for us; we are made in God's own image and likeness but God does not intend for us to be clones of God — all perfectly the same without any distinguishing differences.

All the features of the life of Jesus, even the ones that appear most insignificant, are like beautiful strokes in the portrait of love or like the beautiful notes from the various instruments in a magnificent symphony of love. But Jesus was not just a nice guy floating around the countryside making everyone feel good. From the very instant of his conception to his ascension into heaven he struggled against the forces of evil that battle against the reign of love. Jesus lived this life of love in many ways that were often as inspiring as they were scandalous to those formed and conditioned by the many distortions of a sinful world. He inspired the people with the authority of his beautifully liberating teaching, which went far beyond what they had heard from their teachers and elders. Just take time to read and contemplate the Sermon on the Mount beginning in the fifth chapter of St. Matthew or in the sixth chapter of St. Luke, and this will become obvious. He turned the values and priorities of the sinful world upside down. But this was not without dangerous consequences. He often risked his life, and at the end lost it because he dared to break what appeared as sacred taboos for the sake of doing good to those in need. Jesus performed many powerful miracles of healing, but the most earth-shaking ones were his welcoming and befriending of the "scum" and rejected of society.

All the features of the life of Jesus, even the ones that appear most insignificant, are like beautiful strokes in the portrait of love or like the beautiful notes from the various instruments in a magnificent symphony of love.

It is amazing how easily and quickly good people are shocked and scandalized when anyone goes beyond their notion of goodness — like inviting ex-prisoners and street people to a social gathering. Some of my good parishioners were scandalized when they realized that some of the prostitutes were coming to church. "You should drive them away, Father. They make us look bad," they would tell me. When I would ask, "Do you think Jesus would have driven them away," they would simply walk away in silence. Radical goodness is still scandalous to many of the good people of society. We quickly forget that Jesus, and today we his followers, came not to condemn but to invite to new life. While many saw the defects, Jesus saw the goodness of people. Jesus shocked the crowds when he refused to condemn the woman caught in adultery. It is not difficult to imagine what all the self-righteous people were commenting among each other. He did not hesitate to visit with women and children — considered a silly waste of time in his culture — and went even further by inviting women into discipleship, thus affirming the full dignity of women. When he dined with publicans, tax collectors, and public sinners, he dared to cross forbidden boundaries because of his unlimited love of people and his desire to bring people together. When he exalted the publican — an outcast of his society — he was exposing the hypocrisy of its leadership.

He was gentle and kind with the lowly, suffering, and excluded while being harsh with the arrogant and self-righteous; he was serious, yet could be fun-loving as he appears to have been at the wedding feast of Cana. He was equally comfortable with the lowly and the mighty because he loved them all; he was comfortable with the crowds and his own inner group, but he needed to refuel by going off into the mountain to pray and be alone with his heavenly father — the one source of his unlimited love. This communion with the unlimited and unconditional love of God enabled Jesus to face criticism, rejection, threats, and even death. Because he lived in perfect communion with God who is love, human threats could not stop him from loving others and introducing the ways of love into a calloused, self-righteous, and hate-driven society. The price would be great, but it would be worth it. Love is not cheap and not everyone is willing to pay the price, but the prize is beyond earthly measure or human expectation.

> The kingdom of God is like a merchant in search of fine pearls, on finding one pearl of great value, he went and sold all that he had, and bought it. (Matt. 13:45)

But love is not without pain and sacrifice — both for the lover and for the beloved. In fact, sacrifice is one of the core elements of true love, for by its innermost nature, true love is self-giving. For most of us, however, letting go is difficult and painful. "For whoever wishes to save his life will lose it, but whoever loses his life for my sake will find it" (Matt. 16:25). One of the great misconceptions of today's culture of instant gratification is that people think there can be love without sacrifice, that there can be love without pain and tears, that there can be love without a self-emptying for the sake of those we love. This is more the imprisonment and blindness of self-love than the liberation and vision of true love. This type of self-love leads to one of the great heresies of our times: that everyone has an unlimited and unconditional right to happiness, regardless of what happens to others. It is true that the right to the pursuit of happiness is a fundamental right instilled within us by the creator, but the fundamental question is "What is happiness?" Is happiness just getting what I want? Is happiness just living a life of leisure and pleasure? Is happiness just having wealth, power, and stardom? Happiness is much more than all these.

In the epistle to the Philippians, St. Paul tells us to put on the attitude of Christ, who did not consider being of divine condition something to be clung to, but emptied himself, became like other men, even unto death on the cross (Phil. 2:5–11). It is only in the innermost attitude of giving ourselves to others that we will come to the experience of true happiness. It will not always be fun, it will not always be exciting, it might be painful, and could even lead to the ultimate expression of love: that we give our life for the sake of others. Yet it is only in this attitude of total giving that true love will be experienced. We see it in many ordinary ways in people who sacrifice for the sake of their children, for the sake of their elderly parents, for the sake of orphans and abused children, for the sake of the poor and the homeless. In a heroic way we see it in persons like St. Maximilian Kolbe who during the Holocaust gave his life so that another might go free. We see it in the life of Oscar Romero, who sacrificed his life for proclaiming the truth, and in the Maryknoll sisters and Father Stanley Rother of Oklahoma, who were murdered in Central America for helping the poor to develop agriculture so that at least they would have simple nourishment. Whether it is sacrificing the comfort of a good night's sleep for the sake of caring for the baby to entering into martyrdom for the sake of others, it is through sacrificial love that we obtain what the heart most desires: true and authentic love that is the fundamental basis of lasting happiness. Love is the most beautiful thing there is, but it is never cheap. It is the most precious gift we can ever give, yet money cannot buy it because it is more costly than all the money in the world.

Love is not necessarily popularity. Everyone loves to be popular and well liked but sometimes true love demands unpopularity. "If the world hates you, be aware that it hated me before it hated you. If you belonged to this wolrd, the world would love you as its own" (John 15:18). There is nothing more difficult and painful for loving parents than to have to correct and sometimes even punish their children, yet without this, the children can easily go astray and end up destroying themselves. Coaches who know and value their players are quick to correct their errors precisely because they believe in them and want to bring out the best in them. So it is with God throughout the Bible, especially evident in the Old Testament. Because sin had so distorted our human values and priorities, God had to constantly correct and even punish the people to get them on the right path. I am sure that sometimes the people might have experienced anger and disgust because of God's punishment, yet in the end they end up praising God because they realize that it is precisely because of God's loving care that punishment was necessary — not to destroy them, but to set them on the right path.

In clarifying the nature of love, Jesus gradually adds other elements or, we might say, other strokes to the painting that portrays a truly loving person. The entire life of Jesus is a portrait of the being, words, and actions of a truly loving person. The narratives of the Gospels bring out various aspects of love in action. Mary is the first example when after the discovery of her pregnancy, she forgets herself and travels the dangerous road to assist her elderly cousin Elizabeth (Luke 1:19), very much like parents who forget their own troubles and fatigue to be there for their children. This was also the case of Peter's mother-in-law, who got up from her illness to minister to Jesus and his friends (Matt. 8:14–15). Joseph is willing to disregard the tradition of his time and possibly even be ridiculed by his family and friends by taking the pregnant Mary into his household as his wife. He risked ridicule in order to protect the dignity of Mary (Matt. 1:18–25). This is very much like persons who are willing to hire ex-prisoners in order to reintegrate them into society with dignity.

The good Samaritan (Luke 10:25–37) is a classic example of one who spontaneously goes out of his way to reach out to a stranger in need, very much like persons in the Peace Corps and other such groups who go out of their way to reach out to those in need. The woman who washed the feet of Jesus and anointed them with great care and tenderness (Luke 7:36–47) is another moving example of true love, very much like those who work with the sick and the elderly, carefully washing and dressing their wounds. Lazarus, Martha, and Mary, who offered friendship and hospitality to Jesus (John 11), are very much like those working in homeless shelters offering dignity, friendship, and hospitality to the poor. The merciful father who runs to greet his returning disgraced son (Luke 15:11–32) is very much like people in Alcoholics Anonymous who go out of their way to joyfully welcome disgraced and wrecked alcoholics trying to make a comeback into sobriety.

Other beautiful examples of love in action include the case of the young man with the few pieces of bread (John 6:9) who is willing to give up the little he has so that others will not go hungry. Out of the young man's generosity Jesus is able to feed the entire crowd.

Charity is not about giving what we don't need, like the clothes we no longer wear or the food that has been sitting in our pantries. True charity is about giving even what we need so that others who have less may not go without. Charity can be seen in the women who left their homes to accompany Jesus (Luke 8:1–3) and even finance his mission, very much like professional men and women who leave their lucrative professions behind to join religious orders or lay groups dedicating their lives to working for the poor. Charity can also be seen in the women and the beloved disciple who stood by Jesus at the cross when everyone else had deserted him (John 19:25–27), very much like those who are willing to stand up for a just yet unpopular cause — like standing up for, sheltering, and defending the undocumented immigrants in our country as the people in the Humane Borders organization are doing by providing water in the desert for those risking death to find work in the United States. Many people have been persecuted and insulted because they dared to offer sanctuary to poor people who had sought refuge in our country. Finally, like Joseph of Arimathea and Nicodemus (John 19:38) who took the body of Jesus to be buried, we see the work of Mother Teresa and many like her who not being able to change the scandalous structures of injustice, at least help the poor and the destitute to die with dignity and receive proper burial.

But the best example of true, authentic love is Jesus himself. He is the infinite and unconditional love of God made flesh in order to enter into intimate communion with us human beings. The entire life of Jesus is a journey of charity, of love in action, of sacrificial love for the sake of others. The more we reflect on the life of Jesus as presented in the Gospel narratives, the more we discover that the only way to truly appreciate authentic love is through the life of Jesus, and the only way we can truly know Jesus is through the optic of unlimited love.

Doctrine: A Service of Love

The life of a person is beautiful, but it can be easily misinterpreted in many ways. Jesus did not want his life or his message to be distorted or misinterpreted. Hence he promised the spirit of truth to his apostles. They, and bishops as their successors, would not only proclaim the good news of Jesus, but would safeguard its integrity and guard it from false interpretations. It was not for them to invent new teachings, but to gradually delve into the full meaning of the words and deeds of Jesus and to interpret them with authority as the Gospel goes from one generation to the next and travels into new territories. Gradually the doctrine of the church evolved into, not an imposition, but a service of charity and a guarantee that in our enthusiasm we will not distort the true meaning of Jesus.

Chapter Four _____

Obstacles to Charity

Disfigured by sin and death, man remains "in the image of God," in the image of the Son, but is deprived "of the glory of God," of his "likeness."
— *Catechism of the Catholic Church*, no. 705

A SON MIGHT PHYSICALLY be just like his father, but his behavior might be totally different; hence one could say "you are the living image of your father, but you are certainly not like him at all." Every human being, regardless of ethnicity, social class, or even religion is created in the image of God, but not everyone lives out the likeness of God, who is infinite love. In this chapter I'd like to explore some of the obstacles to love and some of the deviations that I have experienced in my own life and in the lives of others. We are all born into a world whose knowledge, values, and priorities have been confused and sometimes totally distorted by sin. Yet sin could not destroy the innate desires of the heart that have been placed within each one of us by the creator. It is of the innermost nature of the human heart to desire freedom, recognition, success, loving relationships, and happiness. Yet the big question is: How can we truly fulfill the desires of the human heart?

I know there are many how-to books that offer to lead us to fulfillment and happiness, and I have no doubt they offer very good advice and have helped many people, but for the Christian believer, the answer is quite simple: love!

> I give you a new commandment: love one another. As I have loved you, so you also should love one another. This is how all will know that you are my disciples, if you have love for one another. (John 13:34–35)

It is clear that love is the way to the fullness of life, but it is not that easy to love given our human condition. It is true that we have been reborn in Christ and have begun the pilgrimage to eternal life, but between what has started in us and the achievement of our final goal of eternal life in heaven there will always be a large gap and a constant struggle. There are many obstacles to the life of charity, but one of the roots of many of them is in our own insecurity due to our inadequate knowledge and appreciation of God and of ourselves. The ultimate basis of our infinite worth, dignity, and beauty is that we are created in the image of God, who is love, and our great challenge is to live out the likeness of God; the sadness is that because we lost the likeness of God, we don't recognize or appreciate ourselves or others for what we truly are. This leads to low self-esteem and self-centeredness in some while others might suffer from the opposite extreme with an exaggerated notion of their own dignity and self-worth. This can happen to persons as well as entire nations that fall into the idolatry of nationhood (*Catechism of the Catholic Church*, no. 57). A healthy self-knowledge and self-appreciation come from the proper relation between ourselves as creatures and

God as our creator who created us in God's own image and likeness.

Low self-esteem is very painful and destructive and has many debilitating effects. It is a very lonely and isolated prison that conditions and limits much of our thinking and behavior. It keeps us from appreciating our own selves, from recognizing our abilities, and thus from even trying to develop the talents God has given us. When we are convinced that we are worthless, inferior, and incapable, we will not even try, and all the potential that is within us for doing good will be totally wasted, not because we are selfish but because we are convinced we have nothing to offer. Very painful consequences can easily flow from a low self-image, including envy, resentment, sarcasm, and even hatred. Yet it can also ignite a drive to succeed, to get ahead, to prove oneself. This is certainly good but can easily lead to the idolatry of success at any cost, hardening one's heart and sensibilities to the needs of others.

Envy and resentment destroyed the brotherly relationship between Cain and Abel and caused Cain to murder his brother. Ever since then it seems that rather than appreciating ourselves in our uniqueness we need to compare ourselves to others. Rather than striving to become the best possible self, we struggle to become better than others. Envy can have many harmful consequences leading to self-destruction and the destruction of others. Many of the very popular Spanish-language *telenovelas* constantly bring out the disastrous consequences of envy as it leads to lies, intrigue, ugly gossip, betrayal, and even murder. When we are envious of someone, we allow that person to totally dominate our lives. We become blind to our own talents and possibilities because we are so obsessed with the talents and possessions of the other. Envy keeps us from discovering and appreciating our true self and often generates anger and frustration. But envy can also arise out of a sense of misdirected love, a love that is focused on material attachments such as clothing, jewelry, cars, computers, a house, and any number of material things. Our consumer society creates so many needs that we often feel deprived if we are not buying the latest item that the commercials convince us we need to be acceptable.

One of the greatest contributions a parent, teacher, or true friend can make is to help us discover the talents we are endowed with and begin to develop them. A good parent and a true teacher, especially in the primary grades when the core personality is being formed, will seek to help the children discover and develop their God-given talents, never classifying children as better or worse but helping each of them to develop in their uniqueness. One of the greatest talents of a charitable person is the ability to see talents and possibilities where others see only defects and deficiencies. This was certainly my own case. When I started school, I spoke only Spanish. Because I could not understand what was going on or even speak up in class, I hated school. I would spend most of the class daydreaming, doodling, and just looking out the window. I was very lonely and would find ways of going off by myself because I couldn't converse with the other kids — they would make fun of my English. I would have loved to just drop out of school but my mother would not let me. Finally in the fifth grade a nun took a special interest in me and started showing me that it could be exciting to learn and I could not only do it, but do it very well. This completely changed my life — from failing grades to all A's. One person helped me discover what I was capable of. It was like a complete rebirth into new life.

Probably a much greater obstacle to the practice of charity is self-centeredness or selfishness, especially as it has been conditioned by our individualistic, materialistic, and hedonist cultures. When I am constantly thinking of myself and believe that the whole world exists for my pleasure, I become deaf and blind to the needs of others around me, and even if I notice them, I remain indifferent to their needs. We become slaves to our emotional drives, centered exclusively on our need for pleasure and immediate satisfaction. Even worse, the superficiality of our desires suffocates the most authentic desires of the heart so that we strive for passing fancies while ignoring the true treasures of life that will never fade, the ones that will lead to lasting joy and happiness. We find it difficult and even impossible to enter into authentic relationships of love because there will be too many other distractions to allow true love to flourish.

Other obstacles to the practice of charity are arrogance, self-righteousness, and legalism. Arrogant persons are so preoccupied with exhibiting their own importance and superiority that they will not even notice the needs of others, hear their cries, or see their misery. Arrogance makes one haughty, proud, demanding, pushy, and hateful. It takes great charity to be able to love arrogant people, for they are too much in love with their own arrogance to allow people to lovingly enter into their inner lives. Arrogance can be a characteristic of a person, but it is even more damaging when it is the characteristic of a particular human group, a society, or an entire nation. Arrogance gives one the feeling and conviction that one has the right to use others for one's own benefit.

This can easily lead to the enslavement and exploitation of others, the legal classification of others as inferior, and even the destruction of others because they are deemed unfit to live. This characterized the early European contacts with the Native Americans and is still the case in many places. Native Americans are still considered inferior and are exploited throughout Latin America. The Nazi regime's extermination of Jews, homosexuals, gypsies, people with terminal illnesses, and Jehovah's Witnesses was "justified" because they were judged unfit to live, a poisonous element that needed to be eradicated.

> *The law is not always a true compass of good morals and can even become a mask for social immorality.*

Righteousness is good and noble: to live in accordance with the ways of God. The truly righteous person lives in the gratitude that it is God who has transformed us from lawlessness and hatred into loving and righteous persons (Rom. 3:30). It is not that we have made ourselves good through our own efforts and good works; it is God who has made us good. The ultimate expression of true righteousness is the love of neighbor (1 John 3:10). True righteousness is uplifting while self-righteousness is repulsive. Self-righteous persons tend to ignore the grace of God and rely on their own efforts. This was the problem with the Pharisees, who were good and sincere people but had lost the sense of the very purpose of the law (Luke 18:9–14). Self-righteous persons tend to be so concerned with doing the right thing that rather than being charitable they become judgmental, rather than lending a helping hand, they lash out with a condemning tongue, rather than recognizing the need, they criticize the needy, rather than uplifting the fallen, they stomp upon them. This is sad. They strive so hard to be good, even depriving themselves of legitimate pleasures, that they end up being very unhappy persons. This was the case of the older brother in Luke's story of the merciful father and the prodigal son (Luke 15:11–32).

Legalists are so concerned with the externals of the law that they fail to see that laws can be created to defend sinful structures, for example, the laws that legalized child labor and slavery. True law should protect everyone, especially the weak, who are unable to protect themselves from the abuse of the powerful. Yet today many of our laws are carefully crafted to protect the interests of the large business conglomerates rather than protecting ordinary people — families, the sick and infirm, children, the elderly, and most of all the poor of our society. In a sense this is the perversion of law for it protects the interests of the powerful at the cost of legally exploiting the masses of the people. That is why the law is not always a true compass of good morals and can even become a mask for social immorality. Legalists can easily hide behind the law to ignore the cries of the poor. This has certainly been the case in recent times in the immigration debate. The emphasis on "law" has not only ignored but refused to recognize the true nature of the situation. When you combine arrogance, self-righteousness, and legalism, as can easily happen in the dominant and powerful societies and even in the religions of the world, personal acts of charity will still be possible but will often be condemned as illegal and subject to punishment.

Two of the most common obstacles to charity are laziness and sloth, certainly interrelated but not exactly the same.
The lazy person simply does not want to do anything while
the slothful person simply doesn't care. The lazy person sees
what needs to be done but is too tired to do anything about
it, while the slothful person sees what needs to be done but
doesn't care or doesn't want to be bothered — "Let some-
body else take care of it." The lazy person does not want to
be bothered by other people, for they appear as a nuisance
to be avoided. Sloth and laziness lead to a numbing of the
senses, a draining of energies, and an absence of desire. In
many ways such persons appear to be the living dead. It is
true that what appears to be laziness might rather be a biological or psychological condition that causes fatigue, such as
a hormone deficiency or depression. But it can also be a state
of mind that destroys the human spirit. For lazy and slothful
persons, charity is beyond their perceived realm of possibilities. It is no wonder that the early scholars of Christianity
considered sloth one of the seven deadly sins: like the other
capital sins it engendered other sins and vices.

One of the great tragedies of people who get used to living on welfare is that laziness becomes their ordinary way
of life. It is true that welfare programs are absolutely necessary in many circumstances, but it is equally true that some
who really don't need them get used to being taken care of by
others and refuse to make an effort. In such cases the most
charitable thing to do is to find them meaningful employment.
Franklin Roosevelt did just that during the Great Depression,
and as a result not only did many people find meaningful
employment, but great projects were undertaken throughout
the country that beautified the environment. This was a great

welfare project, for it helped the unemployed not by giving them handouts but by offering them the opportunity to be involved in productive work while earning a living wage. In my own city of San Antonio, some of the most beautiful places we have today, such as our famous River Walk, were built through those programs. I admire many of the poor immigrants I have met who do not want a handout but the simple chance to work.

Another of the great obstacles to a life of charity is deeply buried within our contemporary culture, which has identified happiness and fulfillment with having a good time, with doing all the fun things you can manage, being entertained by good foods, good drinks, good sex, good trips, and good games, and generally seeking pleasure without end as if fun and games was the ultimate goal of life. It is not bad to relax and enjoy life, but making enjoyment the all-important dimension of life keeps us from being aware of our own innermost needs and the needs of others. It's good to enjoy a good ball game with friends and family, but the obsession of following sports even to the point of neglecting family and others can be destructive. A pleasure-centered life makes healthy human relationships of friendship, love, and concern very difficult and even impossible. Love cannot be put into action in a truly fulfilling way if our love for pleasure is greater than our love of persons.

Another element of our culture that is a deep obstacle to charity is our growing inability to forgive. It seems that people insist on justice, punishment and satisfaction as a coverup for their desire for vengeance. People seem to think that punishment is necessary to heal offended people. "Make them pay for it!" The escalating numbers of persons in our detention centers, prisons, jails, and death row is one of the darkest and most alarming aspects of our American society. We are a country of law and order, but I wonder if law and order is not sometimes used as an instrument of revenge. Sometimes people express deep dissatisfaction because they consider the penalty imposed by a judge as too soft. This spirit of vengeance and retaliation clouds the mind, embitters life, and destroys love.

Our contemporary society emphasizes upward mobility, being number one, artificial physical beauty as the measure of human worth, material prosperity, maintaining the youthful and sexy look forever, and instant gratification. At the same time it puts the practice of charity on a very slow back burner. The competitive drive can easily deaden our senses to the needs and cries of others, even of those we love the most.

We need to be in constant activity and we transmit this to children — from school to Little League, to swim class, to ballet, to quick supper, to tutoring, and on to other activities. We get busy in so many seemingly demanding activities that we just can't seem to find time to be concerned about people. Our many activities even keep us from being aware of many of the things that are happening around us. I remember how deeply moved I was several years ago when I heard a tearful, young person singing, "Are you listening to what I am not saying?" People around us might be sending signals of pain, but often our many distractions keep us from noticing them. People are good and want to be good. Americans respond generously to people who have suffered disasters, yet in ordinary everyday life our many pressures and multiple activities often make it difficult to even think of being charitable.

Sin: Misdirected Love

Adam and Eve loved the lure of material things more than they loved God; Cain loved his own importance more than he loved his brother; the people of Babel loved their own greatness more than they loved God. Misdirected love leads to horrible consequences.

The *Catechism of the Catholic Church* states:

> Sin is an offense against reason, truth, and right conscience; it is failure in genuine love for God and neighbor caused by a perverse attachment to certain goods. It wounds the nature of man and injures human solidarity. It has been defined as "an utterance, a deed, or a desire contrary to the eternal law."
>
> — *Catechism of the Catholic Church,* no. 1849

Chapter Five

The Fruit of True Freedom Is Charity

For freedom Christ set us free; so stand firm and do not submit again to the yoke of slavery.   —Galatians 5:1

I T IS A FASCINATING paradox that only through obedience can we become truly free, and only through freedom can charity erupt spontaneously — not as an obligation but as the deepest desire of the human heart. Freedom is the child of love and in turn gives birth to a loving heart. But freedom and love are intimately connected to a liberating obedience. Obedience is the doorway to freedom, and charity is the fruit of true freedom. This sounds a little crazy, doesn't it? How can I be a free person if I have to obey. And you might well ask, Can't a slave or a servant be charitable? Can't children who have to obey their parents or teachers be charitable? As a matter of fact, a person who appears to be free might actually be very enslaved while slaves might be even freer than their masters. The world we have created for ourselves lives under many illusions, and one of the greatest is our false notion of freedom, often leading to multiple enslavements of the mind and the heart.

One of the greatest confusions of our times, and probably of all times, is that freedom means doing anything I want to do. This becomes the downfall of the powerful and the source of frustrations and disappointments. It leads people into destructive actions and ruins what could be beautiful relationships of love and friendship. Such confusion enslaves us to the tiny prison of ourselves and can only lead to frustration, emptiness, jealousy, anger, and even violence in the case of gangs and wars in the case of nations. Obedience seems contrary to freedom, and we oppose one to the other. In our culture of individual rights we think of obedience as the negation of our inherent right to do as we please. Obedience sounds like a bad and dehumanizing word. We equate an obedient person with a subservient one, one who has given up his or her free will and is completely dominated by another. Our western culture, which glorifies the individual who goes out to conquer the wilderness, considers obedience as the opposite of freedom — the freedom of the gunmen who are laws unto themselves. We seem to think that we have to obey when there is no chance of doing our own thing. Obedience for the sake of obedience seems so dull and enslaving. Some even feel that obedience is a constraint of the human spirit that kills initiative and creativity. But if obedience were only a passive compliance to the will of another, it would destroy one of the most beautiful qualities of human beings: the ability to be creative, to think of new possibilities, to make new discoveries, and to embark on new adventures. So, as we hope to show, obedience is much more than passive and uncritical compliance to the will of another.

But it is not just our culture that predisposes us to have an intense aversion to obedience. It goes much deeper than that. "For just as through the disobedience of one person the many were made sinners, so through the obedience of one the many will be made righteous" (Rom. 5:19). Once sin had entered the world through disobedience, then rebelliousness, stubbornness, defiance, and meanness subdued the likeness of God in the human sprit. Henceforth obedience would be regarded as a weakening of the human drive to be fully human through power and might rather than through love. Because of the deformities caused by sin, humanity was robbed of true life. It was enslaved by false values, blinded by confused knowledge, and crippled by inordinate desires.

Our entire society goes into shock waves if people are not buying. People are not content with being; they seem to have to be buying in order to stay alive, and if the nation is not buying, it seems to be dying.

This corruption has often had brutal consequences. Just witness the massive cruelties of recent times — many of them committed in the name of development and progress. The Americas witnessed the enslavement or elimination of the native peoples and the suffering of Africans who were forcibly brought to America. Today we hear of the incredible numbers of young people and women who are sold into prostitution. Not too long ago, we witnessed the Holocaust in Germany as the Western world maintained silence. Today thousands are killed as a consequence of the drug trade. The natural resources of the poor countries are depleted for the sake of the enrichment of the wealthy. Poor peoples, especially undocumented immigrants, continue to be exploited. As Pope

Benedict XVI consistently points out, both Marxism and capitalism have failed humanity by converting human beings into mere expendable commodities. The great economic powers claim to be working for a free world while in effect they are enslaving the masses in a world of unrealizable material goals and impossible expectations. They promise a heaven on earth through material gains alone. Even if this could be partially realizable, it will never be truly fulfilling. Our capitalistic society will never deliver on its promises, and thus it leads to deeper frustration and new forms of violence.

I know a young pilot who flies the wealthy in their private jets to the most luxurious resort places in the world. His one observation that remains constant is that they never really enjoy the man-made paradises they fly to. They seem to have everything anyone could possibly desire and yet they seem to enjoy nothing at all. People become enslaved by the desire for luxury and pleasure, only to find that it is never truly fulfilling. And the worst part of it is how many have suffered silently through hard labor and deprivation so that a few might be materially wealthy while being spiritually deprived and humanly deformed.

Descartes said, "I think therefore I am." I think that the common philosophy today is: "I buy therefore I am." Our entire society goes into shock waves if people are not buying. People are not content with being; they seem to have to be buying in order to stay alive, and if the nation is not buying, it seems to be dying. When buying slows down, the president calls an emergency gathering of experts, but when people are dying before their time because of poverty and lack of medical care, nobody seems to care. Sometime ago we had some neighborhood sports and arts programs in one of the poor areas of San Antonio. One afternoon some of the young people asked to speak to us. They were very gracious, but they explained to us that as good as the programs were, they needed more. They needed to make some money because if they did not have some pocket money to buy a cold drink or a burger, they were nobodies. "Without a little money to spend, we are nothing." We have equated being with having, happiness with possessions. We use people while loving things.

It is true that there are certain types of obedience that curtail and even destroy our innate quest for freedom. There is enslaving obedience when we simply have to follow orders whether we like them or not, whether we understand them or not, whether we approve of them or not. The result of this kind of obedience is usually bitterness, indifference, and even a sense of defiance. This does not lead to true freedom. There is likewise a demanding obedience that rather than enslaving leads to creative freedom. This is the obedience demanded by a caring parent, teacher, or coach who strives to educate the person through the discipline necessary to form the right values and patterns of life. Once these values and patterns have been interiorized, the person is free to creatively put them into practice. Each one of us is born with many talents, but they will emerge and come to fruition only through guidance, encouragement, challenge, and discipline. This type of obedience, rather than enslaving, leads to a creative free expression of our talents. This is where the Ten Commandments come in. They are God's gift to a rebellious humanity to ensure a proper way of relating with one another without always being threatened by the other. You might say they are the starting point, the basic discipline that will prepare us for the ultimate commandment: love one another.

There is another type of obedience that masquerades as freedom: the need for conformity. This is the desire to be myself within the context of the demands of my society. I claim to be myself, to dress as I want, to do what I want, but in reality I have accepted the programming imposed on me by society. It is amazing how much the fashion industry manipulates us into conformity even as they project a certain type of individuality. Even young children are manipulated into wanting only a certain name brand of shoes, clothes and accessories. Take, for example, the need to be beautiful in accordance with the dictates of the fashion magazines, or the need to look eternally young. Society conditions us in many more ways than we can imagine, and we become imprisoned by its norms and dictates. We live in the illusion of freedom when in effect we react like well-programmed robots.

There are, however, other kinds of obedience that are very liberating. When I obey medical experts, I am free from having to study medicine, and by following their instructions I share in their expertise. The same is true when I follow the advice of other experts. This type of obedience frees me to develop my own talents. Because no one of us can be an expert in everything, although some might act as if they are, we all need to share in the expertise of others to complete our poverty. You might say that this is the obedience of the mind: I freely consent to the instructions of the expert whose wisdom and knowledge I trust.

But there is a higher and more liberating kind of obedience: the obedience of the heart. When I love someone, I freely and willingly want to do what he or she wants to do, and when I know that person loves me, the trust is without question and the obedience truly fulfilling. Even though I might not understand others completely, I trust the ones I love and want to enter into communion with them by making their will my own. When the obedience of the mind is combined with the obedience of the heart, we begin to experience the most liberating kind of freedom, and this is the kind of freedom from which charity flows as naturally as water does from a spring. When we love others and trust their knowledge and wisdom, we freely want to enter into communion with them, to share in their lives, to follow their counsels, to joyfully do what they want us to do.

Yet in life even this type of obedience can be deceiving. Even with the best of intentions my lover can be mistaken and unintentionally lead me astray. The best of human love and confidence can still fail us, but divine love and wisdom never will. The most liberating obedience comes when there is absolute confidence in the knowledge and authority of the beloved. This was the love that Jesus had for the Father and the Father for the Son, and it is into this communion of love that Jesus invites us through the gift of the Spirit. It was this unquestioned love and confidence that enabled Jesus to be freely obedient even unto death on the cross. "I love the Father and do as the Father has commanded me" (John 14:31).

Here is the mystery of this paradox of freedom through obedience that results in charity. Humanity had turned away from God and in seeking to be free on its own terms had actually fallen into a multitude of enslavements. Yet the quest for freedom and fulfillment still remained deeply rooted in the human heart. God so loved the world that God gave his son that we might be liberated from the enslavements of the heart, regain our true sense of freedom, and by living out that freedom obtain life in abundance. In obedience to the Father's love (Phil. 2:6–11), Jesus came to restore humanity to its true self as intended by the creator and to reveal to us the truth of what ultimately makes us authentically human and allows us to live in the true freedom of God's children. "For just as through the disobedience of one person the many were made sinners, so through the obedience of one the many will be made righteous" (Rom. 5:19). Through his obedience, the nature of true freedom would be revealed, the only freedom that leads to authentic fulfillment of the heart's desire for freedom. In him, we find the truth, the way, and the life, that is, the only true way of achieving human fulfillment (John 14:6). In him, love, obedience, and freedom are one. It is in this triangular relation of love, obedience and freedom that man and woman can achieve the fullness of life and the true harmony, peace, and happiness that the human heart so insistently longs for.

The Son, in obedience to the Father whom he loved, lived a life of love for others in complete freedom from any societal forces that hinder human freedom. His intimacy with the Father gave him a wisdom and freedom that was truly astonishing and liberating. Do a quick reading of the Gospel stories and you will quickly discover this marvelous freedom of Jesus. He was free of the control of his parents: "Did you not know that I must be in my Father's house" (Luke 2:49); free of the expectations of his friends: "Get behind me, Satan. You are thinking not as God does, but as human beings do" (Mark 8:33); free of the pressure of political authorities: "Go tell that fox [Herod]" (Luke 13:32); free of the demands of public opinion when he invited the rejects and "impure" of society into his company and even dined with them (Mark 2:13–18). He was not intimidated by earthly authority (John 18:28–19:22). He was free of the limitations of his culture and religion: "You have heard the commandment, . . . but I say to you" (Matt. 5:1–7:29). He was free to love the humanly speaking unlovable, to care for the widows, foreigners, and orphans and to invite into his company the despised and "unclean" of his society. No wonder people criticized him as being a "glutton and a drunkard, a lover of tax collectors and those outside the law" (Matt. 11:19). Because of the unquestioned love of his Father, he was free to love others regardless of the cost — even when it cost him the distrust of his family (Mark 3:21), his reputation (Mark 3:22; 12:22), the abandonment of his disciples (Mark 14:50) and even his life by death on the cross.

His entire life was a triumph of love. That is why St. John calls this the hour of his glorification, because even the agony of the cross could not force him to stop loving us. The ugliness of an enslaved humanity could not destroy the beauty of a totally free person. Obedient in order to be free. This was the obedience that made Jesus radically free to love without hesitation or limit. His obedience made our freedom possible. He was obedient to the Father to introduce into humanity the freedom of unlimited love. His entire life, from beginning to end, was a life of sacrificing love for the sake of bringing us to life. Like the love of a mother who sacrifices herself that the child might be born, so Jesus sacrificed himself that the new humanity of love might be born. Not only that, he gave us the Spirit to enable us to be liberated from all enslavements so that we too could love as he loved.

The obedience that the New Testament speaks about is not the external obedience demanded by legal systems. This type of obedience to law is necessary for the good ordering of communities and societies so that people can live in relative peace and tranquility, but it does not produce the freedom of the spirit that overflows in charity. In fact, as St. Paul brings out in the epistle to the Romans, it can actually lead to wrath (Rom. 4:15). It can also lead to resentment, anger, and hypocrisy. The key to appreciating the liberating obedience of the New Testament is given by Paul when he speaks about the obedience of faith, that is, the free desire of a lover to live in perfect communion and harmony with the beloved.

Faith is a gift of God that arises out of our encounter with the living Lord and my acknowledgment of him as the Lord of my life, as the true friend who will never lead me astray, as the one who put down his life for me and for all of us. "No one has greater love than this, to lay down one's life for one's friends" (John 15:13). Because I believe in him I trust him, and having experienced his love, I love him in return. In his divinity I can trust him completely and without hesitation, and in his humanity I can truly seek to follow his way and to walk in his footsteps. Because I love him, I want to do his will. Even though at times it may seem difficult and even irrational, my love and confidence urges me from within to do his will. Jesus never said it would be easy. In fact he invited us to take up our cross and follow him. But he did promise us that lasting peace, joy, and happiness that God alone can give (Matt. 16:24–28).

The obedience of faith is the obedience of the mind and the heart, the obedience of love. This is why the so-called "law of Christ" can be much more demanding than any human law would dare to be, yet at the same time be much more liberating than any law is capable of being. "Love is the fulfillment of the law" (Rom. 13:10). It is in the following of Christ, who in his loving obedience to the Father lived a life of perfect freedom, that we ourselves are free from the many enslavements of the world and may enjoy true freedom. Jesus knew this would be difficult, so he gave the Spirit to all who are reborn in him so that we too might call God Father and live as his children.

> As proof that you are children, God sent the spirit of his Son into our hearts, crying out, "Abba, Father!"
>
> (Gal. 4:6)

In the epistle to the Galatians, St. Paul gives us a beautiful description on the fruits of true freedom that results in charity:

> For you were called for freedom, brothers and sisters; only do not use your freedom as an opportunity for self-indulgence, but through love become slaves to one another. For the whole law is summed up in a single commandment, "You shall love your neighbor as yourself." ... The fruit of the Spirit is love, joy, peace, patience, kindness, generosity, faithfulness, gentleness, and self-control. There is no law against such things. And those who belong to Christ Jesus have crucified the flesh with its passions and desires. If we live by the Spirit, let us also be guided by the Spirit. Let us not become conceited, competing against one another, envying one another.
>
> (Gal. 5:13–26)

St. Paul carefully enumerates various aspects of charity that flows from Christian freedom. You will notice that the first fruit of the spirit is love, followed by joy and peace. There is nothing more life-giving, joy-producing, and peace-establishing than the experience of being loved unconditionally. It is amazing. God, who knows me with all my qualities and faults, calls me by name and invites me into intimate friendship with God and other human beings (Vatican Council II, Constitution on Divine Revelation, no. 2). The recognition that I am a lovable and desirable person produces a deep sense of joy and peacefulness.

But it does not stop here. Because I am at peace with myself, I will have the ability to be more patient with others even in the most difficult circumstances. It is the patience that enables me to walk along with others in their difficult and even intolerable moments and be a source of strength to them. It is the patience that enables me to maintain my composure and dignity when being ridiculed and even insulted by others, never lowering myself to their ugly standards. This was the patience that enabled Jesus to go through all the ignominies and humiliations of his passion without giving in or ever losing his composure. Closely related to patience are gentleness and self-control.

For those who have experienced the totally gratuitous and undeserved love of God, kindness, generosity, and faithfulness will be as natural as the air they breathe. They will always treat others as if they are the most important and precious person in the world. After all, that is the way God treats me. Charity is not a matter of just being charitable once in a while or when I encounter someone in need. It is about consistency in the everyday activities of life. It is about treating others with respect, valuing their work, recognizing their abilities, being generous in the quality time we spend with them, bringing joy and understanding into their lives. Faithfulness to God's great gift of love allows me to continue growing in the ability to love others as God loves. This is not a one-time affair but a lifelong adventure leading me through experiences I could never expect or predict. The love of God is the greatest and the most exciting of all human adventures. It is full of many unexpected surprises, and the greatest of all surprises only will come at the end!

Among the beautiful and edifying aspects of charity are gentleness and self-control — the ability to treat others with dignity and respect regardless of who they are or what their social status might be. This is a clear manifestation of a self-confidence that is not threatened or frightened by others. One does not have to be haughty, insulting, domineering, or arrogant to demonstrate power and authority. True authority does not have to be authoritarian. Gentleness and self-control do not mean that I simply have to agree with everything others say or do. It is the ability to be firm without being insulting, to be able to disagree without being disagreeable, to be able to correct without embarrassing. Charity is the ability to remain gentle and in self-control in the midst of the most difficult circumstances. A great example of this marvelous quality of a truly free and charitable person is the behavior of Jesus throughout his trials with the Sanhedrin, Herod, and Pilate. His gentle but firm composure and dignity towered over the nervousness and insecurity of his adversaries.

The profound desire to be a free person is one of the deepest and most beautiful drives of the human heart and equally one of the most mysterious and complex. True freedom is creative while false freedom is destructive. In biblical terms we would say that sin is freedom gone astray. Thus the more we know and love God, especially through Jesus of Galilee, the more we will strive to exercise our freedom to be creative of new and better forms of life. This involves every human activity from working for better family relations in the home, school, workplace, and church to the discovery of new foods and medicines that will alleviate the sufferings of humanity. By uniting our creative activity to the work of Christ we are, even if we are not aware of it, participating in the redemption of the entire universe. In the liberating obedience of the heart and the mind, we will obtain the greatest degree of fulfillment possible in the realization that just as God created out of the chaos, so we too are creating new life for others and even for our world.

If you remain in my word, you will truly be my disciples, and you will know the truth and the truth shall set you free. (John 8:31–32)

Moral Codes: Safeguards of Freedom

Freedom can easily be misguided and lead to destruction of self and of others. True freedom is beautiful, inspirational, and creative, but a false sense of freedom leads to the destruction of self, family, society, nations, and the earth itself. God gave us the Ten Commandments as the first steps toward inner freedom: to be able to live in a society where every person respects the rights of others. We are created by God to live in society, but we cannot live in peace and harmony if we are always against one another. Jesus went further in taking us from basic obligations to the ideals of the law of love that results in true freedom. As society advances and becomes more and more complex, the church as a loving mother and teacher is there to help freedom remain on the path of true love. The moral teachings of Christ and his church are not an imposition or even a limitation of freedom but rather a guide to ensure the true exercise of freedom.

Chapter Six _____

The Effects of Charity

J ESUS GAVE US the example of charity not only through his
own lifestyle and that of his followers. He also gave us
the Spirit to enable us to live the new life of charity in our
daily lives, even to the extreme of heroic dedication. It would
be St. Paul that would bring out clearly the various elements
of the primacy of charity in the life of Christians. Nowhere
is this more clearly expressed than in his first epistle to the
Corinthians, chapter 13:

> If I speak in human and angelic tongues but do not have
> love, I am a resounding gong or a clashing cymbal. And
> if I have the gift of prophecy and comprehend all mys-
> teries and all knowledge; if I have all faith so as to move
> mountains but do not have love, I am nothing. If I give
> away everything I own, and if I hand my body over so
> that I may boast but do not have love, I gain nothing.

I think that if St. Paul were writing today, he would expand
his litany to say: if you are the greatest ballplayer of all time
but do not have love, you are no better than a circus baboon;
if you are the greatest performing artist but do not have love,
you are no more than a fancy puppet; if you have become the
wealthiest person in the world but do not have love, you are
no more than a massive garbage dump; if you are the most

noted academic or scientist but do not have love, you are
no more than an educated parrot; if you are the most erudite
theologian or preacher and do not have love, you are no more
than a skillful shyster. It is simple. The true measure of human
greatness and success is our ability to love and especially to
love those in greatest need. But sometimes the greatest test is
to keep loving those who are the closest to us, those whom
we have loved the most. This is why in St. John's Gospel Jesus
no longer tells us just to love our enemies; now he tells us to
love one another. Sometimes this is the hardest thing to do.

The only true measure of human success is love, and without it even the ones who appear to be the most successful are
nothing more than the cloud that appears great and powerful in the morning but has disappeared by the afternoon. The
only true basis of lasting happiness is love, and without it isolated moments of happiness quickly fade into sweet memories
of the past. The divine love that I experience in my heart is
not just the beautiful love of one person for another; it is the
love of God within me that now animates and guides every
moment, every feeling, every thought, every desire, and every
action of my life. Whether I am dealing with the person whom
I love the most in this life, with a stranger, or even with an
enemy, it is the love of God within me that will be the driving force of my life. The more this love grows within me, the
more I can say with St. Paul: "I live no longer I, but Christ
who lives in me" (Gal. 2:20).

St. Paul then goes on to give us some of the characteristics
of love in action, of the truly charitable person:

> Love is patient, love is kind. It is not jealous, [love] is not
> pompous, it is not inflated, it is not rude, it does not seek

its own interests, it is not quick-tempered, it does not brood over injury, it does not rejoice over wrongdoing but rejoices with the truth. It bears all things, believes all things, hopes all things, endures all things.

(1 Cor. 13:4–7)

To begin with, "Love is patient." Patience is not a placid feeling or the lack of emotions; rather it is perseverance under trials and tribulations, even the most intense ones, without giving in or just quitting. It is maintaining a positive attitude under painful circumstances of discouragement, trial, or temptation. "This is the patience of the saints" (Rev. 13:10). Patience, however, can be good or bad, depending on the reason for our patience.

If you are the most noted academic or scientist but do not have love, you are no more than an educated parrot.

Sometimes we have no choice but to be patient, like when we have been sitting in a plane awaiting takeoff for a long time and are finally thanked for our patience — did we have a choice? Or waiting on the phone while listening to the weird music until the voice of an attendant finally comes on, that is, if we are lucky enough to get a human voice and not just another recording. Sometimes it is not a matter of patience but simply of not having a choice.

"Love is patient." This sounds easy and simple, but it can be difficult in everyday life especially when we have to deal with persons who love to make life miserable for us. Sometimes no one can do this better than those that we have loved the most. It is amazing throughout the scriptures how God was patient with the errors and deviations of his people and continued to find ways of saving them. In the scriptures, patience is always related to hope, for it is hope that enables us to endure the sufferings of the present in the assurance of better things to come.

> My heart is overwhelmed, my pity is stirred. I will not give vent to my blazing anger, I will not destroy Ephraim again; For I am God and not man, the Holy One present among you; I will not let the flames consume you.
> (Hos. 11:8–9)

> Return, rebel Israel, says the LORD, I will not remain angry with you; For I am merciful, says the LORD, I will not continue my wrath forever. (Jer. 3:12)

It was not infrequent that God was tempted to destroy his people, but out of love, his patience prevailed. Job is an example of heroic patience. Jesus too dealt with his adversaries with great patience and calls upon his disciples to face persecution and adversity patiently. He even reproaches his disciples when they want to call down fire and brimstone upon the unbelieving towns (Luke 9:54–55). The early Christians waited patiently for the coming of Christ in all his glory, yet it never happened.

It is interesting that St. Paul begins with patience, probably because he knew well from his own experience how difficult it is to live with one another, even with those we love deeply. We often speak of community but frequently find it difficult to put up with each other. We tend to be petty and easily disturbed by whatever does not go our way. This happens between persons as well as between corporations and nations. Somehow, we seem to think that our way is God's way and that everyone else should march to our tune.

Thus love implies being patient with ourselves and with others. It means being tolerant and accepting of differences. It means being willing to hold back on our quick temper and tantrums. Even more than that, true charitable patience gives us the wisdom and the courage not to be destroyed by others even when they insult, ridicule, and persecute us. We can rise above the insults and injuries of others and pray that they might be delivered from whatever is causing them such poisonous anger and destructiveness. Once we give in to the anger and insults of others, we begin our own self-destruction. Thus patience is even a way of self-preservation. If I follow the example of Jesus, no amount of insult or injury can force me to stop loving others. This is charity at its best.

The most difficult and yet the most liberating aspect of patience is forgiveness. A truly patient person finds the courage to forgive injuries and insults in the hope that the very forgiveness will bring about the conversion of the offender. Forgiveness does not mean that the pain of the injury has disappeared, for the scars will always be there. But it does mean that with the help of God's grace, my love for others is greater than the pain inflicted by them. This was the power of Jesus on the cross.

St. Paul goes on to mention the second characteristic of love: "love is kind." Kindness implies generosity, concern, benevolence, loving care, compassion, and forgiveness. Kindness is the virtue that moves us to treat others as God treats us. A truly kind person is a living icon of the very selfhood of

God. It is one of those qualities that make a person truly beautiful and attractive. A truly kind person radiates the beauty of God. Generosity is not just about being generous with the things that we have; even more it means sharing our very selves and our talents with others. It means having time for others, time to listen to them, time to pray and recreate with them, especially those who are lonely and neglected.

But kindness is also about benevolence, that is, thinking well of others, and this implies the ability to see the good in a person, even when others see only the negative. You might say that the virtue of kindness is a positive prejudice in favor of the other. The kind person can see the beauty and dignity of others, even those considered insignificant and undignified by society, and treat them with respect and courtesy. Such a person can sense the needs of others and reach out to help them before they even dare to ask. Another characteristic of kindness is the ability to rejoice with others in their good fortune.

We all know that life is not a continuous joyride. There are many disappointments and tragedies throughout our lives, and the pain is great when we have to suffer alone with no one to accompany us. In some mysterious but beautiful way, suffering is lessened when there is someone to accompany us. One of the life-giving aspects of kindness is the virtue of compassion, that is, being able to share in the suffering of the other. Compassion does not mean that I approve or even understand; it simply means "I am with you, you are not alone."

Sometimes we come to know what something is by paying attention to what it is not. This is exactly what St. Paul does as he goes on to describe love by what it is not. "It is not jealous, it is not pompous, it is not inflated." What a marvelous summary of what love is not! One of the beautiful traits of charity is not only that we rejoice in the good fortune of others, but that we ourselves are not pretentious or overbearing. Jealousy is not only a constant discomfort; it is one of the great enemies of charity, for jealous persons will be so consumed with loathing the qualities and possessions of others that they will never have time to see or appreciate the pains, sufferings, and needs of others. Self-centered persons tend to speak only about themselves while charitable persons will be comfortable with a good conversation, listening and speaking with simple words.

The scriptures, however, speak of a jealous God which could lead to some confusion: "You shall not worship any other god, for the Lord is 'the Jealous One'; a jealous God he is" (Exod. 34:14). The difficulty arises because the Hebrew term for jealousy is used in different ways. Here it refers to the diligence that is manifested in guarding conjugal chastity. In this sense it is profitable for us not only unhesitatingly to admit, but thankfully to assert, that God is jealous of his people when he calls them his wife, and warns them against committing adultery with a multitude of false gods. A jealousy that springs from love is one that is zealous in guarding the welfare of the loved ones; it is intolerant of infidelity. This is the jealousy St. Paul speaks about in 2 Corinthians 11:2: "For I am jealous of you with the jealousy of God, since I betrothed you to one husband to present you as a chaste virgin to Christ." Such a jealousy is the virtue that safeguards the harmony and unity of human relations. Clearly it can become inordinate and dangerous when it is fueled by irrational suspicions or fired up by malicious gossip, but in

itself it is a virtuous quality that arises out of the intensity
of love and concern for the good of others and is solicitous
of their welfare. A better English term for this type of jealousy might be a "passionate concern" for the welfare of those
we love.

On the other hand, the jealousy that St. Paul is constantly
speaking about is the one that arises out of envy and resentment (see, for example, Gal. 5:19–21; Rom. 1:28–32; and
1 Cor. 9–10). This is the type of jealousy that is the basis of sin
itself. St. Augustine called it a "diabolical sin" because from
it flowed hatred, detraction, calumny, joy at the misfortune
of others and displeasure at the prosperity of others.

Jealousy was the reason for the entry of sin into the world,
and it has become ingrained in our sinful nature. Adam and
Eve fell because they could not appreciate who they were or
what they had because they wanted to be what they were
not — like God. They had already been created in the image
and likeness of God, but because they wanted to become even
more, they ended up becoming less. Cain could not appreciate
his own gifts because he was so obsessed with the blessings
of his brother, Abel, that he killed his brother. Jealousy is a
root cause of many injuries, betrayals, and even murders.

> While there is jealousy and rivalry among you, are you
> not of the flesh, and behaving in an ordinary human
> way? (1 Cor. 3:3)

The inner freedom of charitable persons will enable them
to remain calm and poised in the midst of the most disturbing
circumstances. As St. Paul states: "Charity is not rude." The
ability to be respectful of others, especially of our subordi-
nates, is a marvelous quality of charity. It is the recognition

that every person we encounter is of infinite worth and dignity regardless of their status and position in society; so we treat others as if we were speaking personally with God. Sometimes you meet people who are very polite and respectful with those who appear to be superior to them yet they become despotic with those who appear to be inferior to them. Charity allows us to deal with any person we meet in a dignified and respectful way.

Another important aspect of charity is that "it does not seek its own interests." This goes contrary to our upward mobility, self-centered mentality in Western society. Our modern culture, with its many marvelous traits, nevertheless has the negative one of putting one's self-interest before anything else. You often hear people say: "I have a right to my happiness" — totally ignoring the needs of all others. The tragedy with this mind-set is that we gradually close ourselves into the prison of our own self and use even the most beautiful of human relations just for our own self-fulfillment. This might lead to many achievements but it will never lead to a truly lasting happiness.

Charity regulates our daily relations with others. As St. Paul states: "It is not quick-tempered." In everyday life, this can be one of the most important elements of charity. Keeping calm can be very difficult, especially when dealing with troublesome persons. It becomes a primary virtue for parents bringing up children and for anyone who has to work with others, especially nurses, teachers, caregivers, and other similar occupations. A quick temper is a spontaneous and emotional response to an unpleasant and aggravating situation. It can easily lead to disastrous consequences such as uttering ugly, insulting, and destructive comments that easily destroy even

the most beautiful relationship. I have dealt with many mar-
riage cases where the root of the problem started with an
exchange of insulting words. A quick temper can easily lead
to stupid actions, cost a person's job, or even provoke the
anger of others: "Those are fighting words!" I've often heard
people say: "Calm down or you're going to do something
crazy." Many domestic disturbances and even stabbings and
shootings are caused by the quick temper of someone who
will later on claim "temporary insanity."

This does not mean that we do not have a temper and that
our temper will not flare up on occasions. In fact on occasions
of gross injustice and crimes, it should flare up and move us
to action. Jesus did not hesitate to be upset with his disciples
when they failed to understand him (Matt. 15:16 and Mark
7:18) nor with the temple vendors who were exploiting people
in the name of God (Matt. 21:12–13; Mark 11:15–19; Luke
19:45–46; John 2:13–17). The point that St. Paul makes in
this remark is that it should not be "quick" — that is, that we
should be careful not to blow up at ordinary inconveniences
and difficulties, nor to let our emotions drive us to actions we
will later regret. I'm sure St. Paul would agree that an even
temper is closely related to prudence and is a quality of the
charitable person. An even-tempered person can contribute
greatly to the maintenance of harmony and peace in all human
situations.

The next characteristic of charity reflects a deep perception
of our human condition: "It does not brood over injury, it
does not rejoice over wrongdoing but rejoices with the truth."
Injuries of one kind or another are part of life. We don't wish
them upon anyone, but they happen at the playground, at
home, at work. To live is to get hurt. And sometimes the

greatest pain is the knowledge that we have hurt someone we love. Hurt is very real and can be quite painful. Yet the greater pain is the inability to get over it. It even keeps us from sleeping and eating well and drives us to make life difficult for others. St. Paul warns us clearly: "Be angry but do not sin. Do not let the sun set over your anger, and do not leave room for the devil" (Eph. 4:26). Holding on to grudges is not only exhausting but, even worse, it results in bitterness, negativity and the inability to enjoy life. Again this is why St. Paul exhorts us: "All bitterness, fury, anger, shouting, and reviling must be removed from you, along with all malice" (Eph. 4:31). Brooding over past injuries drains us of energy and keeps us from living life to its fullest while making life miserable for others.

There are people who seem to delight in brooding over past injuries. They even seem to enjoy reopening the wounds of the past, thus making life miserable for themselves and everyone around them. One of the great qualities of a charitable person is the ability to accept misfortune and move on with life, not allowing injuries to destroy life. I love the prayer of AA: "God, grant us the serenity to accept the things we cannot change, courage to change the things we can, and wisdom to know the difference." Some wounds of the past can be healed, but others we simply live with and do not let them dominate or destroy our lives.

In a perverse sort of way, some people find healing in their enjoyment of the misfortune of others. This sadistic sense of humor adds further injury and humiliation to the injuries of others. If it is beautiful to be able to laugh with others on occasions of merriment, it is insulting and degrading to laugh at the misfortune of others. Charity does not enjoy the misfortune of others nor does it take their misfortune as occasions for self-glorification.

"It bears all things, believes all things, hopes all things, endures all things." Whoa! This is a daunting goal to live up to. In Spanish, one of the great virtues is that of *aguante,* which could best be translated into English as "endurance" or maybe even "relentlessness." We stay the course no matter the hardship or the obstacles. In the context of the entire Christian message this is a very positive trait. This is not a passive attitude of indifference but a dynamic strength of perseverance. God has started the new life in us but we need to cooperate with God to bring it to perfection. This will never be easy, and there will always be distractions and deviations. Take a moment to read about the things St. Paul went through (1 Cor. 11:21–32), yet he remained steadfast because, as he tells us, "[the Lord] said to me, my grace is sufficient for you, for power is made perfect in weakness" (2 Cor. 12:9).

As we carry on in life, not letting our sufferings and afflictions disturb us and even offering them for the sake of the world, we are participating in an amazing sort of way in the redemption of the world. "Now I rejoice in my suffering for your sake, for in my suffering I am making up for what is lacking in the suffering of Christ" (Col. 1:24). The great French Jesuit scientist Pierre Teilhard de Chardin used to write to his paralyzed sister, who was bedridden, telling her how the free offerings of her sufferings were doing so much more for the sake of humanity than all his scientific writings — and he was one of the greatest scholars of his time. He used to say that the first challenge of suffering is to work to eliminate the causes of the suffering, for suffering is an indication that humanity

still has a lot of work to do in perfecting the world and the
people God has entrusted to our care. Yet in the present moment, suffering that cannot be eliminated can be united to
the suffering of Christ for the redemption of creation. Charity is using all our creative abilities to eliminate the causes
of hunger, disease, homelessness, malnutrition, exploitation,
and slavery; it is using our creative abilities to safeguard and
protect the environment; it is using our creative abilities in
finding better ways of relating that eliminate hatred, abuse,
indifference, and prejudice and provide for a better distribu-
tion of wealth among all people. Yet at the present time we
are living in the tension between the redemption of all creation that has begun in Christ and its completion at the end
of time. We do all we can to bring about change, but we accept the inevitable sufferings that cannot be eliminated and
unite them with the sufferings of Christ, knowing without
doubt that in some mysterious way they will be efficacious
in the redemption of creation. This is precisely why St. Paul
could say about his suffering: "I rejoice in my suffering for
your sake" (Col. 1:24).

I can certainly attest to this deep mystery from the many
years of my pastoral experience. I have seen sick people
become demanding and despotic while I have seen others
become caring and compassionate toward their caregivers.
I have seen that people who can capture a deeper meaning in
their suffering seem to transcend the physical pain and rather
than being a source of pain for their loved ones, they become
a source of comfort and inspiration. Rather than demanding
attention and care, they delight in offering comfort to those
who visit them. In the midst of their agony they radiate a joy

and peacefulness that is truly contagious. In their hearts they know that in their suffering they are participating in the great work of redemption; by their suffering they are united in a special way to the suffering of Jesus on the cross.

Believing all things does not mean that we are so naïve as to believe anything. Believing all things here refers to believing everything Christ has taught us; it means believing the entire Christian message and not just the parts that we like while ignoring the others. Even when we, like some of the first followers of Jesus, find his sayings to be hard and are tempted to depart from him (John 6:60), we can say with St. Peter: "Master, to whom shall we go? You have the words of eternal life. We have come to believe and are convinced that you are the Holy One of God" (John 6:68–69). But "believing all things" is also a challenge to keep growing and deepening in our understanding and appreciation of the things we believe. The more we love others, the more we want to know all about them and the more we know about them, the more we can love them. So it is with God through Jesus. "The love of Christ surpasses all understanding" (Eph. 3:19). So "believing all things" is the natural quest of a loving person. Only through a lifetime of reflection on the life and message of Jesus can we gradually enter into the knowledge that surpasses all human understanding. This is definitely not a call to irrationality but rather a recognition that through faith we go beyond the limits of human rationality into the rationality of love.

Because of our faith in God, we know that all things will work out well at the end for those who love God. "We know that things work for good for those who love God, who are called according to his purpose" (Rom. 8:28). Trials and tribulations cannot set us apart from the love of God (Rom. 8:35), and our confidence in the providence of a loving God will keep our hopes up even beyond all human expectations. Hope is the basis of enthusiasm and can drive people to exciting adventures. It is not just the hope for immediate results for material things — like the hope of winning the lottery, winning a ball game, or landing a good job. To hope in better things in life is not bad; in fact, a life without hope is bleak. But Christian hope goes beyond that to a hope in the things to come — good things that are beyond the human mind to even imagine: "Eye has not seen, ear has not heard, nor has it entered the human heart what God has prepared for those who love him" (1 Cor. 2:9).

"Love never fails. So faith, hope and love remain, these three; but the greatest of these is love." A simple summary statement of the absolute guarantee of charity: the beautiful, multiple, and diverse effects of charity will not fail to bring about peace and joy, harmony and tranquility, happiness and serenity. The cost and the sacrifices might seem great, but the result will be far beyond our ability to measure.

Chapter Seven _____

Jesus

The Source and Summit of All Virtues

I am the vine, you are the branches. Whoever remains in me and I in him will bear much fruit, because without me you can do nothing. —John 15:5

The Longing of the Heart

C HARITY IS NOT JUST one good deed or another; it is not just almsgiving; it is not just reaching out to one in need. These and a million other good deeds are certainly good and beautiful effects of charity, but charity is much more. Charity is allowing the life of God to work through our ordinary, and sometimes extraordinary, deeds and words of daily life whether in the home, at the airport, in the grocery store, at work, or in the world. The source and summit of charity is God, and we encounter God personally in the person of Jesus of Galilee. All creation comes out of God's love, for God had no need to create, and much less to create creatures in God's own image and likeness. God existed in perfect happiness and beauty, but precisely because God is love, God wanted to share this perfect joy with others. Thus God created. Creation and humanity come from the heart of God, and they will reach their ultimate perfection when the beloved come to complete communion with the lover.

My mother immigrated to the United States from Mexico at a very young age. She and her mother came from Mexico City by train. She learned to love the United States and never talked about returning to Mexico. During the rest of her life, she had very little contact with Mexico, except for visits from relatives who occasionally visited my hometown of San Antonio. Yet during her final days on earth she became nostalgic about returning to Mexico City by train. Sometimes I would come home in the evening and she would be anxious about going to take the train to Mexico. The only way I could calm her down was to tell her today's train had already left, but we could go the next day. In her dying days she was anxious to return to the place of her origins.

It is beautiful to see how during major holidays or personal events such as weddings, baptisms, and funerals people are eager to return home to be reunited not only with family and friends but also with the landscape and familiar surroundings of the homestead. Immigrants who come to the United States from Mexico, the Philippines, Vietnam, and other countries often make great sacrifices to return home for special events and even just vacations. Often immigrants like to place a bit of the old sod in their new country by building churches like they had in the old country, opening restaurants that serve their traditional food, and organize celebrations like they had back home. Ethnic food sections have become very popular in the grocery stores of our multi-ethnic America. Sometimes immigrants want their bodies returned home for burial after they die. Even if they had left because of misery and horrible conditions, they still often speak sentimentally of the home country as a lost paradise. People whose ancestors immigrated to new lands generations ago are often nostalgic about making a visit to the "home country."

I remember a good friend of mine who is a university professor making a trip to the small town in northern Italy from which his grandparents had emigrated. He was totally "Americanized," yet he felt an inner calling to visit the land of his origins. He didn't know any Italian, and it probably would not have helped him if he did because in that small town people spoke a dialect quite unique to the mountain area between Italy and Austria. Yet when he arrived, he managed to communicate and actually find elderly people who remembered his family and were able to take him to the home where his father had been born. They even went to the local parish and found his baptismal record. I remember visiting with him upon his return, and the excitement that he exhibited was beyond the words he could find to explain it, even though he was a very popular conference presenter who was never at a loss for words. He said he really could not explain the deep feeling of being connected with what seemed like ultimate reality, like being connected to the very roots of his existence.

Even though I very much know San Antonio as my hometown, I remember very well the first time we visited the small hamlet where my father had been born and raised in northern Mexico and then when we visited my mother's birthplace in the great and ancient metropolitan capital that is Mexico City. The contrast between the small hamlet and the glowing capital was striking, yet the deep feeling of returning to the place of my origins was equally profound, nostalgic, and even sacred in both places. I knew instinctively without anyone having to explain it to me that I was in contact with the earthly origins of my existence. Was this an expression of a desire for something much greater and primordial?

It is no wonder that "homecoming" celebrations are major attractions that bring people from distant places, while restaurants like to promote the fact that they serve home-cooked meals. As we grow up, especially in today's world of easy and quick mobility, we go in many directions, finding new friends and forming new networks of relationships. Yet there is something deep within us that secretly longs to be united with our origins, with our roots, with the ground of our existence. Even if we had difficult experiences growing up, there is still a spark buried deep within our psyche that pulls us toward the place of our origins.

It seems that it is within our very makeup that we have the need to be connected to that from which we have come, to be in touch with our earthly roots. Could this quest for origins be indicative of something much greater than we dare imagine? Could it be the whisper of our desire to be in contact with the ultimate root of our existence and eventually be reunited with our origins? I remember both my father and mother in their final moments calling out to their mothers, to the womb that had given them life, and their dying desire to be reunited with this place of origin.

We come from God who is love, the source of goodness and beauty, and our final destiny is to be reunited with God in love. God is love! God-love is the source of our life and our ultimate goal.

> The kingdom of heaven is like unto a treasure hidden in the field, which a man found and hid; and in his joy he goes and sells all that he has, and buys that field.

Again, the kingdom of heaven is like unto a man that is a merchant seeking goodly pearls: and having found one pearl of great price, he went and sold all that he had, and bought it. (Matt. 13:44–46)

Long before human beings started to think of God as a male figure, they thought of God as a pregnant woman.

My friends who are biblical experts tell me that the Hebrew word for "compassion" actually means a mother's trembling womb — trembling to create life, trembling to give birth to life, trembling to protect the life it has created, and trembling to receive life upon the completion of its journey. We come from the womb of God, the womb that is trembling to let go of the life it has created. But once new life has been created, a good mother is ready to let go, while encouraging the child to go forth on the adventure of life, giving the child the luxury of making its way through life. When the child makes mistakes, even tragic ones, the mother will be saddened and even angry at times but will not cease loving the child and hoping for the best. Throughout life, the mother longs for the return of the child.

Can a mother forget her infant, be without tenderness for the child of her womb? Even should she forget, I will never forget you. (Isa. 49:15)

I often tell people on Mother's Day that the greatest gift they can give their mother is to have the family together around her. In many powerful ways the image of a mother's trembling womb — to release what it carries within while anxious about its welfare and longing for the return of the life it has given — is a reflection not only of the origins and goal of our life but even more of the ultimate source and goal of charity. We come from the dynamic love of God and our hearts will not be content until through love we are reunited with God in our true homeland, which is heaven.

One of the oldest human depictions of God is that of a mother. Long before human beings started to think of God as a male figure, they thought of God as a pregnant woman. The womb was the dark, mysterious, and sacred cave where life was created. From the earliest dawn of human beings upon earth they sensed that God was the author of life. But it took biblical revelation and especially the person of Jesus for us to come to the realization that God is not only the all-powerful and mysterious creator of life but also the passionate lover who not only creates but gives us the ability to love as God loves. In loving like God we recuperate the likeness of God that has been lost through sin. The infinite goodness of God is visible throughout creation but it became fully manifested in the life of Jesus. God is love. This love is made visible in Jesus, and through him it is offered to us. Jesus invites us to come to him, for he alone can quench our deepest thirst: "The water I give shall become a fountain within them, leaping up to provide eternal life" (John 4:14). He alone can lead us to the fullness of life. He is the source of our ability to love without limit, and union with him will lead us to the highest summit. We allow his life to become our very own through contemplation, celebration, and communion.

Contemplation

It is no wonder that medieval Christian writers contemplating the nature of all things described the roots of charity in God's love for humanity. Charity is God's active, dynamic, and creative love for creation and humanity. It is rooted in the very nature of God: the Father's love begets the Son and their mutuality of love begets the Spirit. The Trinitarian relationship itself is one of sharing and giving, not out of necessity but out of desire. The very core of Christian revelation is about God as relationships of love and the perfection of God as infinite and endless love.

It is not just that God gives. It is the very way that God gives and the extent of this giving that reveal to us the truth of what giving out of love implies. God's love, as the scriptures bring out, is mysterious, compassionate, intimate, joyful, passionate, enthusiastic, patient, and long-suffering. It is warm and caring. It is personal: God loves *me*. It is communitarian: God loves us ("Give *us* this day our daily bread"). Sometimes God's love is clear and evident while at other times it seems to be totally absent. Yet we as believers who have tasted of this love know that it is always there. I'm sure this must have been the experience of Jesus during the agony in the garden, the passion, and the crucifixion. Sometimes we are at the peak of the mountain, as Jesus was on Mt. Tabor, while at other times we might seem to be in the pits of hell, as Jesus was on the cross when he cried out: "My God, My God, why have you abandoned me?" (Matt. 27:46), yet we know that our God never abandons us: "Father, into your hands I commend my spirit" (Luke 23:46). How do we know this? As the great theologian St. Bonaventure would tell us: "by gazing on and contemplating the crucifix" and, I would add, "by gazing on and contemplating the manger."

Much of our knowledge comes from reading, and study, but the deep knowledge of the love of God cannot come through study and reading alone, even through the study and reading of the scriptures. Much more is required. For us to enter into the depth and breadth of the mystery of God's love for us, prayer and contemplation are the necessary gateways. It is through them that we enter into the vast universe of the world of pure and unlimited love. This is the contemplation of lovers who simply by gazing upon one another experience a deep communion with one another and a profound compenetration of each other's lives. No words are needed or even wanted, as they might break the mystical bond that communicates what spoken or written words are incapable of fully expressing. This is why contemplation on the images of scripture leads us into an experience that will make the words of scripture come to life within us. Through contemplation, the written word now becomes the living word of life within us, and we experience much more than the words alone could ever express. The words by themselves cannot substitute for the experience but the experience without the words can remain ambiguous and even misleading. We are so used to reading books that in many ways we have lost the sense that it is through contemplation that we go beyond what we read into the depths of the mystery of God who is love. We have often heard that a good image is worth a thousand words. I would say that a good image of the divine actions in history is worth more than many good books could express.

Even after God's chosen people consistently deviated from the ways of God and even rejected God, God kept loving us and wanting to rescue us. The story of creation, sin, and redemption is the dramatic and fascinating story of a lover who keeps reaching out to the beloved even when the beloved continues to ignore, ridicule, betray, and insult the divine lover. The extent of God's love for creation and humanity goes far beyond the powers of human reason to comprehend. "Indeed, only with difficulty does one die for a just person, though for a good person one might even find the courage to die. But God proves his love for us in that while we were still sinners, Christ died for us" (Rom. 5:7–8). To die for a loved one is courageous, but to offer to give one's life for one's enemies, for the very ones who have offended you and walked away from you? Through sin we became the enemies of God. Yet God kept loving us to the extreme and refused to abandon us. Only through prayer and contemplation can we begin to have an inkling of the extent of this love. And most amazing is that we are invited to share in this love and thus become lovers like God!

God loved us so much that in time God chose to have the son empty himself of his divinity and become truly one of us (Phil. 2:4–9). He came to accompany us as a fellow sojourner on the way to the promised land. "For our sake he made him to be sin who did not know sin" (2 Cor. 5:21). One does not have to be a sinner to suffer the consequences of sin. Victims are not sinners, but they suffer because of the sin of others. Because Jesus himself was beset with the weight of sin and its destructive consequences for human beings, he would be able to truly understand and appreciate our own daily struggles.

Therefore, he had to become like his brothers in every way, that he might be a merciful and faithful high priest before God to expiate the sins of the people. Because he himself was tested through what he suffered, he is able to help those who are being tested. (Heb. 2:17–18)

He would enter into humanity not as an honorable and powerful potentate according to the standards of a sinful world, but rather as a weak, broken, and humble person, disgraced by the values and standards of a humanity structured and deformed by sin (Heb. 5:2). God became man for our salvation. In becoming man, God became not just any human being, but the suffering victim of the sinful abuses of persons against each other and societies against one another. God would become the victim of the humanly made structures of society that disfigure and destroy the image and likeness of God in human beings and thus relegate them to a status of inferiority, impurity, unworthiness, and exclusion. These sinful structures of society are what the Gospel according to John names as the sin of the world (John 1:29). God became wounded humanity not to make it appear as something good, but to unveil the lie so that human beings might see, recognize, and appreciate themselves for who they truly are and not what the sinful world says that they are. In becoming just such a particular man, God begins to demolish the structures of sin by opening the eyes and hearts of men and women to the truth of God about themselves and about every human being.

Out of this condition of human weakness and frailty, Jesus initiates and reveals a new power unlike any the world had ever known: the power of unlimited and unconditional love: love as concern for others; love as the artisan of a new egalitarian humanity; love as the guiding principle of all our actions; love as the basis of new relationships; love as a passion for life, beauty, and happiness; love as the ultimate norm of our humanness. The entire life of Jesus was fueled by love, a love that even enabled him to accept the humiliation and cruelty of crucifixion rather than turn on us. He loved us even when we ridiculed and rejected him. No human power could force him to stop loving us.

Jesus told us, "Whoever has seen me has seen the Father" (John 14:9). Every detail of the life of Jesus when pieced together is like a marvelous movie of God's love for us: a love that creates, rehabilitates, and invites us to fellowship. The people of the Bible, and we are people of the Bible today, experienced things with all their senses while the words helped them to appreciate the true meaning and purpose of their experience. But even the words that were eventually written down were arrived at through the patient and prayerful contemplation of what had taken place. As we see and contemplate what God has done for us, how God has loved us, our eyes are opened to see much more than we had ever imagined, and in the seeing itself there is an inner transformation that gradually takes place. And what greater events to contemplate than the birth of Jesus in the manger of Bethlehem and his crucifixion at Golgotha. Can there ever be a more beautiful, moving, and powerful expression of the unlimited love of God for us?

Just take a moment to let yourself gaze upon the human reality of the crib and the cross and see what they express about the ugliness of our sinful condition and the extent of God's love. How is it that such sad ugliness can be transformed into such astounding beauty? From within the frightening spectacle the glory of God erupts forth with all the splendor of the rising sun. What appears as a sad scandal is but the beginning of the eruption into our sinful world of God's unlimited love for humanity and all of creation — "We know that all creation is groaning in labor pains even until now ... for the redemption of our bodies" (Rom. 8:22–23). The more we are aware of the many distractions, deviations, and false criteria of judgment caused by sin, the more we will appreciate the depth, the grandeur, the beauty, and the glory of the mind-blowing, heart-warming, and eye-opening extent of God's love for us as contained within the crib, on the cross and everything in between. Is it any wonder that artists never tire of creating new renditions of the birth and death of Jesus. Through contemplation we gradually enter into this awesome and fascinating mystery of love, and in so doing we ourselves will be transformed into divine lovers. God's love became human in Jesus so that in and through him we might become divine.

Celebration

The ultimate sacrifice on the cross, the maximum expression of unlimited love, was prefigured by Jesus himself and given to us as an everlasting memorial in the last supper. This is the great mystery of our faith. He wanted to share this life of total self-giving with his followers. He did this in the most beautiful way possible: through the sharing of a festive meal in which all who partake would be entering into personal communion with him. They would receive his own body and blood, the very life that enabled him to love beyond all humanly imposed limits. Could there be anything more precious and more intimate than one's own body and blood? Nothing is more intimate than a loving touch of the body. A transfusion of blood can give strength to the weak and life to the dying. The final gift would be accomplished on the cross, but we would be able to share in his life-giving sacrifice in a most common and joyful way: a festive family meal.

> Then he took the bread, said the blessing, broke it, and gave it to them, saying, "This is my body, which will be given for you; do this in memory of me." And likewise the cup after they had eaten, saying, "This cup is the new covenant in my blood, which will be shed for you."
>
> (Luke 22:19–20)

From the earliest times, Christians have gathered together to joyfully celebrate the Lord's death, resurrection, and final coming in the context of a fellowship meal — a celebration of love. Throughout the history of the church it has taken on various forms, but the substance has remained the same. Gradually this celebration took on the structure of our eucharistic celebration. The core of the celebration is the proclamation of the words of Jesus over the bread and wine. We prepare for this by recalling the events and words of Jesus. We listen to the word of God in the biblical readings, and through the homily we search for their meaning today. As Catholics we believe that the Eucharist is the source and summit of Christian life. It is through the Eucharist that we participate in the ultimate love of Jesus for us — his life freely given for us on the cross. As Pope Benedict XVI has told us: "The Eucharist draws us into Jesus' act of self-oblation. More than just statically receiving the incarnate Logos, we enter into the very dynamic of his self-giving" (*Deus Caritas*

Est, no. 13). It is the entire unity of the eucharistic celebration — word and sacrament — that draws us into the mystery of Christ. But it is important to remember that the word is expressed not just through reading, but through explanation, songs, and imagery.

If images invite us to penetrate the mystery of God's love through what we contemplate with our eyes, songs lead us to contemplate these mysteries in our hearts. Art and music are not just decorative additions to authentic liturgy; they are essential aspects of the celebration that stimulate our senses and touch our hearts so that we might participate more fully in the great mysteries of God's love.

> Be filled with the Spirit, addressing one another (in) psalms and hymns and spiritual songs, singing and playing to the Lord in your hearts, giving thanks always and for everything in the name of our Lord Jesus Christ to God the Father. (Eph. 5:19–20)

At the recent general conference of Bishops of Latin America and the Caribbean in Aparecida, Brazil (May 2007), they concluded: "It is fundamental for liturgical celebrations to incorporate artistic elements that can transform and help the faithful for their encounter with Christ." Eastern Christians, and to a certain degree Western Christians, and certainly Latin American Christians have always valued the transformative power of sacred images that draw us into the mystery represented. This is an element of our liturgical celebrations that has been missing in recent times. We have relied almost exclusively on the written and spoken word and have ignored the power of the artistic and musical word. All are

essential elements of a communication that will not only il-
luminate the mind but also touch and transform the heart.
Love letters are beautiful, but so are flowers and songs.

Communion

He who eats my flesh and drinks my blood abides in me
and I in him. (John 6:56)

At the peak of the eucharistic celebration we are invited into
a very personal intimacy with Christ by partaking in Holy
Communion. In the reception of the very body and blood of
Christ we encounter the source of our unlimited love and have
a foretaste of what is yet to come: the fullness of life in God. It
is not just nourishment for our journey, although it is certainly
that; it is also the very life-source of our new being, our new
life begun at baptism when we died with Christ to arise with
him to new life (Rom. 6:5–11), the life of dynamic charity
in all circumstances. Communion "preserves, increases, and
renews the life of grace received at Baptism" (*Catechism of
the Catholic Church,* no. 1392).

> This communion, this act of eating, truly represents an
> encounter between two people, it means allowing one-
> self to be penetrated by the life of the one who is Lord,
> the one who is my Creator and Redeemer. The goal of
> this communion is to assimilate my life to his, my trans-
> formation and conformity to the one who is living Love.
> (Benedict XVI, Feast of Corpus Christi,
> May 27, 2005)

The loving care of Christians towards those in difficulty and their commitment for a more supportive society is continually nourished by their partaking of the Eucharist. Whoever nourishes himself of Christ with faith at the Eucharistic celebration absorbs his life style, that is, a style of service geared especially towards the most vulnerable and disadvantaged people. In fact, works of charity are a criterion of the authencity of our liturgical celebration.

(Benedict XVI, World Refugee Day, June 19, 2005)

The deepest longings of the heart will never be fully satisfied until we are fully united with God-Love, the very source of our life. Many good things in this life will bring us partial fulfillment. They can be beautiful and like a foretaste of the final completion. Every act of love brings us closer to divine love and is a participation in divine love itself. God has given us marvelous means of nourishing us with God's own life, especially through contemplation of the mysteries of God among us and by celebration of the Eucharist and Holy Communion. But these should never be an escape from a life of charity. Precisely because of this nourishment, we should be even more committed to a life of charity. As Benedict XVI has brought out clearly, participation in these mysteries is not a substitute for action but rather the awakening of all our senses to be sensitive and responsive to the needs of others, whether they are the ones closest to us or faraway strangers. We are called to serve especially the most vulnerable and disadvantaged of the world.

For those who truly participate in these mysteries, seeking to be of service to others will become more and more of a natural response of the heart. God created the heart for love, and a heart without love withers away into nothingness. A heart without love will seek fulfillment in many ways, but without love, nothing will quiet the innermost desires of the heart.

> God is love ... everyone who loves is begotten of love.
>
> (1 John 4:7–8)

The First Eucharist: The Child in the Manger

The entire history of salvation is summarized in St. Luke's account of the nativity of Jesus. Human beings wanting to be like god order a census of the whole world to build their city and to become divine through military power and conquest. Against this backdrop, we see the poor nameless and homeless couple about to give birth to a child. The shepherds are told that they will find "a child in a manger" — the place where the flock comes to be nourished. The child in the manger is the first sign of the great gift of Jesus: his own body and blood as our nourishment unto eternal life. The census was the symbol of earthly power that uses others for personal gain, while the "child in the manger" is the symbol of the new creation: giving of oneself for the sake of others.

The Challenges of Charity

*Each has a particular gift from God, one of one kind
and one of another.* — 1 Corinthians 7:7

T HERE IS NOTHING more challenging and more exciting
than charity. The spirit of charity guides, regulates, and
stimulates our desires so that they lead us to creative fulfillment rather than to selfish destruction. Because God created
out of love, out of the desire to share God's beauty and goodness with others, love by its very nature is creative. The desires
of love will lead us to many forms of creativity: to create
new life through the conjugal union of love, to create new
possibilities for a better life, and even to create new forms
of protecting and beautifying the environment. Love is not
static; by its very nature it is the fuel of creative energy and
creativity.

Where does love begin? Certainly in the experience of being
loved. But just as plants can rot if they have too much water,
so can life be wasted when excessive love becomes suffocating rather than supportive and stimulating. Precisely because
God is love, we see throughout the Bible how God was a
strong disciplinarian, constantly admonishing and correcting
his people. Jesus, who was infinite love incarnate did not hesitate to correct while inviting his followers to a radically new

lifestyle. I remember visiting a young man in jail who told me that he was in jail because his parents had loved him so much they had given him everything he had ever wanted, but had never given him what he needed the most: correction and discipline. They had offered him suffocating love but not creative love.

A person can be destroyed as much by the lack of love as by too much suffocating love. By creating us in the image and likeness of a creator who brought beauty and order out of the chaos (Gen. 1:1–2), God wanted us to be creative as God is creative. I remember Robert Kennedy saying: "Some see things as they are and wonder why; others see things that are not and ask why not?" We are all born with the creative gene, but it needs to be stimulated, encouraged, and nourished. Childhood curiosity is the beginning of the search for possibilities. Discovery of possibilities is not only exciting but a stimulus to go further. Love, as is evident in God's love throughout the Bible, will be a combination of a call to innovative adventures and ongoing guidance and correction. Beginning with the call to Abraham to leave his homeland, God constantly calls us to new adventures. Because God is a good coach and knows our possibilities, God will be very demanding and work us hard so that we succeed in the most important game of all: the game of life. Correction can be challenging and inspiring without being threatening and destructive. When we love someone and believe in that person, we want to bring out the best in that person. It is misguided never to challenge the ones we love because we fear hurting them.

The most basic starting point of charity is the recognition that God loves me unconditionally; that God loves me as I am, looks at me in my nakedness (without the need of any material adornments), and says, "You are great; you are beautiful." In the radical acceptance of God's love, I realize that I am loveable. God loves and accepts me with my talents and my limitations, and it is the proper balance of both that makes me a perfect human being open to God's graces and to the graces of others.

An important aspect of charity is recognizing the gifts God has bestowed upon me and working diligently to develop these gifts so that I might have something of value to offer to others. St. Paul emphasizes this when he reminds the people: "Each has a particular gift from God, one of one kind and one of another" (1 Cor. 7:7). Unrecognized and undeveloped gifts remain hidden and wasted, while recognized and developed gifts become a great source of fulfillment and satisfaction. Even more than that, they enable us to enrich the lives of others in many different ways. I remember a very poor lady who used to attend Mass at San Fernando Cathedral while I was stationed there. She once told me that she loved to attend Mass at San Fernando "because during the sermons I discover something good about myself that I had never suspected, and I can't wait to go home and put it into practice." This is truly the good news of the Gospel: discovering unexpected talents and activating them or, even more, discovering the dignity, status, and talents society has kept me from recognizing.

At my mother's funeral, a former employee of our family's grocery store came and told me how much my parents meant to him and how much they had done for him. The young man remembered an act of kindness by our dad that changed his whole life. When he was a young boy in elementary school, he was the butt of everyone's cruel jokes because he was tall for his age and mentally slow. One day on his way to school he saw my father sweeping the sidewalk in front of the store and stopped to talk to him. My father complained that because there was a bus stop in front of the store, there was always a lot of trash and no one bothered to sweep it up. The next morning, this young boy got up very early, took his mother's broom and went and swept the sidewalk in front of the store before my father opened the store. He continued to do this for several days until one early morning he found my father waiting for him. My father told him he was so pleased with the job the young man was doing that he wanted to hire him to continue doing it and pay him.

When the young man went to school that day and told everyone that Mr. Elizondo had just hired him to work at the store, everyone was in awe. No other child in the school had a paying job. That afternoon several of his classmates came by the store to see if it was true and if they could get a job too, but my father told them that he had hired the young man because he did such a fine job and he could depend on him. After this, he said, "no one teased me anymore. They all respected me because Mr. Elizondo had given me a paying job." The recognition of his talent had transformed his shame into pride; in many ways, it had given him life.

Recognizing the talents God has given me is only the beginning; much more is needed. You might say that the activation of these gifts with all their potential is my gift to God and neighbor. It is a beautiful way of living out the great commandment: "Love God above all things and your neighbor as yourself." The development of these gifts does not come without disciplined dedication and hard work. It does not come without the guidance of good teachers, coaches, and experts. Yet even the best of instructors will be useless without my own continuous efforts. The development of any talent takes work and dedication. Ask any artist, professional, or athlete. They could never succeed without many hours of disciplined work. God endows us with beautiful talents, but it is our gift to God and to God's people to develop these talents to the best of our ability.

Yet in God's love and wisdom, no one of us has received all the gifts. Imagine what an awesome responsibility if someone were to receive all the gifts and talents possible. It is because of the kindness and compassion of God that we receive only some gifts but never all of them or even too many. Even the most gifted person will be lacking in many ways. I have noticed that persons who seem to be intellectually gifted, such as scientists and university professors, often are emotionally underdeveloped. Yet this is not a deprivation but a precious gift of God to help all of us recognize that no one is better or worse, inferior or superior, gifted or backward but simply all in need of one another. Truly, we are all gifted. To help people discover, appreciate, and develop their own gifts is a great service of charity. To recognize our own poverty, our own lack, disposes us to receive others into our lives.

Thus charity involves the acceptance of my own limitations, rejoices in the gifts of others, and welcomes their assistance. It is fascinating how God from the very beginning of creation has created every individual as a unique creature endowed with specific gifts, yet none is endowed with every gift. This is equally true of ethnicities and nations. To me the great contribution the Hebrew people made to humanity is the recognition that in spite of all the horrible things people thought and said of them, in spite of all the insulting and dehumanizing things they suffered, they recognized that the basis of their existence and their reason to live was that they were God's chosen people. Through them I have come to realize that every people, every ethnicity, is God's chosen people. God does not create something and then reject it. God does not create trash. Every one of us is a loved and chosen child of God.

God created individuals, families, and nations to need one another. One of the beautiful teachings of Christianity is that it is in the very reaching out to one another, both offering what we have and receiving from others what we need, that we enjoy the reestablished harmony destroyed by sin. Sin turned people against each other, causing them to see the talents of others either as threats to their existence, dignity, and honor or as possibilities for exploitation. At other times, we simply ignore people or, even worse, ignore their suffering and close our ears to their cries. At times, our pride keeps us from accepting the assistance of others. Christianity reverses this. Accepting our limitations is not a humiliation, and recognizing the talents of others is not a put-down of ourselves. On the contrary, we rejoice in the various talents that, combined, are the greatest wealth — both spiritual and material — of the community.

St. Paul brings this out clearly when he exhorts Christians to recognize their individual gifts, all for the sake of the community, with gratitude and joy. This is what truly makes us a community of the new creation: each one contributing to the welfare of others and each one receiving from the gifts of others.

There are different kinds of spiritual gifts but the same Spirit; there are different forms of service but the same Lord; there are different workings but the same God who produces all of them in everyone. To each individual the manifestation of the Spirit is given for some benefit. To one is given through the Spirit the expression of wisdom; to another the expression of knowledge according to the same Spirit; to another faith by the same Spirit; to another gifts of healing by the one Spirit; to another mighty deeds; to another prophecy; to another discernment of spirits; to another varieties of tongues; to another interpretation of tongues. But one and the same Spirit produces all of these, distributing them individually to each person as he wishes. As a body is one though it has many parts, and all the parts of the body, though many, are one body, so also Christ. (1 Cor. 12:4–13)

Every people, every ethnicity, is God's chosen people. God does not create something and then reject it. God does not create trash.

We could easily expand on the beautiful words of St. Paul by saying: if you have the gift of music, be the best possible; if you have the gift of cooking, be the best possible; if you have the gift of business, be the best possible; if you have the gift of medicine, be the best possible — yet always for the good of the community, not for ourselves. In the analogy of the body, St. Paul reminds us how even the most insignificant parts are indispensable for the overall health of the person. So it is in society. The important thing is not if one is a great CEO of a Fortune 500 company or the maintenance person of the local elementary school. The all-important thing is how we relate to the betterment of the community.

There is a Gospel parable that, having worked in the hot summers of San Antonio, I never liked: the parable of the workers in the vineyard (Matt. 20:1–16). It just did not seem right nor generous. If the master truly wanted to be generous why wasn't he generous with the ones who had worked throughout the heat of the day? It wasn't until I read the explanation that Vasco de Quiroga of Michoacán, one of the first evangelizers of Mexico, gave to that parable as the foundation of his "evangelical villages" that I understood. He explained that in the kingdom of God, everyone would work according to their abilities and receive according to their needs, and it was usually the ones with the greatest needs who could work the least — the sick and the elderly. This made sense, and it is truly the nature of the Christian community — everyone concerned for the welfare of one another and using their gifts to enrich the entire community.

But charity is also an important challenge to communities and institutions: how to work collectively for the service and betterment of others in a way that respects the dignity of those we are serving. Charity demands a denunciation of the unjust structures of society that deprive people of the basic needs of life. It demands our involvement in movements for better education for children, better health care for everyone, true rehabilitation of those who have made mistakes, the proper care of the environment, just wages and decent working conditions — all areas of life. Society has advanced in many ways, but in many others it is still in urgent need of improvement.

Compendium of the Social Doctrine of the Church: A Guide to Christian Life in Today's World

The *Compendium* is a summary of the teachings of the church on the challenges of Christian living in today's world. It brings out how Christians are to be involved in the issues of society such as the living wage, the treatment of immigrants, the economy, war and peace, the right to life, the right to culture, medical issues, and many other topics of contemporary concern. It is a fine summary of the way the church understands the life of charity in today's world of so many inequalities. Issued by the Pontifical Council for Justice and Peace in April of 2004, it states:

> Love faces a vast field of work and the Church is eager to make her contribution with her social doctrine, which concerns the whole person and is addressed to all people. So many needy brothers and sisters are waiting for help, so many who are oppressed are waiting for justice, so many who are unemployed are waiting for a job, so many peoples are waiting for respect. Christian love leads to denunciation, proposals, and a commitment to cultural and social projects; it prompts positive activity that inspires all who sincerely have the good of man at heart to make their contribution. (No. 5)

Forgiveness
The Ultimate Gift of Charity

Father, forgive them for they know not what they do.
—Luke 23:34

T O ME ONE OF THE greatest mysteries of our human existence and one of the most difficult to comprehend is why human beings who are created by God to love and help one another seem so eager to hurt and destroy one another. Love is so creative, why do we destroy it so easily? Why do we have so many fights in the homes, the neighborhoods, and the world? Why does violence seem to be so attractive and games promoting violence so much in demand? I often tell people that the doctrine of original sin and its consequences is the one doctrine that needs no theological proof. Just listen to the evening news any day of the week or read the daily newspapers: they are dominated by stories of deception, robberies, and crimes of all types. Our country leads the world in the number of citizens in prison. A recent study reported that one out of every hundred adults in the United States is in prison at a cost to taxpayers of $48 billion a year. It is often more expensive to keep people imprisoned than to send them to the best universities. People call for tougher punishment for crime, but no one seems to be calling for radical change in our crime-producing society. Is tougher punishment the answer? Will this heal the crime-producing wave that seems to be ingrained in many societies? Can love prevail over evil?

Love is beautiful but the betrayal of love is devastating. Love is life-giving while abuse is destructive, robbing people of the joy of life and even of life itself. There are many wonderful, kind, and compassionate people in all cultures and religions, but sometimes even wonderful people hurt one another — sometimes intentionally and sometimes without even being aware that they are hurting someone. It is beautiful to see a couple in love preparing for matrimony, but it is painful to see the same couple some time later hurling insults at one another as they prepare for divorce. A most beautiful and moving sight is to see an elderly couple tenderly holding hands after years of struggle together and, in spite of the many ups and downs, loving each other even more than before. They are a powerful witness that true love is possible and enduring. It is inspiring to see diverse peoples working together for the common good or for a common cause, but it is sad and depressing when people turn against each other, fight one another, insult each other, rob, steal, and kill.

It seems that abuse of one kind or another has become the normal way of life. If you are human, you can expect to get hurt, whether in the crib, in the school bus, at home, on the team, at work, or even in church. And even if you are the most wonderful person in the world, you will probably end up hurting someone probably without even realizing it. The pain that comes with the realization that we have hurt someone can be even greater than the pain of being hurt yourself. Learning to hurt others comes with the legacy of sin that we inherit from those who have come before us, but we certainly add to it by our own actions. Is there a way out of this culture of destructiveness? Theologically speaking, how do we break the shackles of sin that seem to have such a stronghold on our cultures?

I grew up with the saying "forgive and forget." It seemed simple and logical, and I had never really questioned it. One day, while visiting the monument to the deportation of the Jewish people and others who had been labeled as "undesirables" in Paris, I was shocked by the inscription over the entrance: "Let us forgive but never forget." This was so contrary to everything I had always been taught. It even seemed to be totally un-Christian. Yet there it was, right in the shadows of the majestic cathedral of Notre Dame.

As I walked through the very somber monument, which resembled a concentration camp, I kept asking myself, "How can I forgive if I am not willing to forget?" Gradually I started to realize that if you can forget, you no longer have to forgive; the real virtue comes when you remember and you can still forgive. Moreover, if you can forget you can easily commit the same faults yourself. Remembering the pain without forgiveness can deepen the pain and evoke deeper feelings of anger and revenge. Remembering the pain with forgiveness can bring healing and a desire to work so that no one will have to suffer what you have suffered. Forgiving while remembering can be an illuminating experience into the depths of human evil without falling into the trap of seeking to correct the matter by committing even greater evils. Remembering without forgiveness can lead to disasters while remembering with forgiveness can lead to new possibilities of life. But is such forgiveness possible?

The very reason God sent God's son to us was to reconcile us to God, to one another, and to all of creation. God wanted to reorient disoriented love, to rechannel the raging currents of our passions from their destructive paths into the proper channels of goodness, compassion, and creativity. God wanted to break the destructive and escalating cycle of revenge by offering us the gift of unmerited forgiveness and love. Throughout the Gospel narratives Jesus speaks of forgiveness that goes beyond what anyone could manage or even imagine as reasonable. This is the great gift of God's love: to bring reconciliation through love: "They are justified [rehabilitated]) freely by his grace through the redemption in Christ Jesus" (Rom. 3:24). The acceptance of the gift, however, does not bring about a magical transformation. It is an invitation to repent and convert: "Or do you hold his priceless kindness, forbearance, and patience in low esteem, unaware that the kindness of God would lead you to repentance?" (Rom. 2:4). The acceptance of God's gift begins the transformation of our minds, our hearts, and all our being so that we are nothing less than a new creation: "So whoever is in Christ is a new creation: the old things have passed away; behold, new things have come" (1 Cor. 5:17). Yes, the old values, priorities, sensibilities, prejudices, viewpoints, and even my entire worldview begin to be transformed. Through the power of the Spirit we have received we begin the struggle of living as Jesus taught us: "I am the way and the truth and the life" (John 14:6). Complete forgiveness is the great gift of God's love. The acceptance of this gift empowers us to forgive because of the divine love that is now alive in us. Forgiveness is never merited; it is a gift of divine love.

Of all the things Jesus asked his followers to do, none is more difficult yet more healing and liberating than forgiveness. Humanly speaking, forgiveness seems impossible while revenge seems sweet and much more natural. It seems that through revenge we can obtain satisfaction, but in reality revenge will never bring about healing. As long as we harbor sentiments of anger and revenge, we will remain imprisoned by these sentiments, thus allowing the very person that offended us to continue dominating our life. We can easily become enslaved by the very ones we would like to destroy.

Sometimes I wonder if the old theological explanations on the necessity of the sacrifice of the cross did not present us with a vengeful God rather than a loving God — as if God's anger could not be cooled until a blood offering had been made in payment for the debt incurred by sin. How horrible! I even remember a classical Good Friday song we sang in Spanish. It was a beautiful melody, but I now realize it had terrible lyrics: "Why are you [God] eternally angry?" I remember hearing in catechism class that because sin had offended the divine majesty only the sacrifice of the divine son could make reparation, as if an angry and fastidious God demanded revenge. The *Catechism of the Catholic Church* clarifies this beautifully when it puts it all in the context of redemptive love — a love that no human force can destroy. Through this love, the sacrifice of the new covenant, humanity is restored to communion with God and one another (nos. 599–618).

The sacrifice of Jesus on the cross was not payment for an offense but a gift of infinite love offered precisely to break the power of the hellish cycle of retaliation. Jesus not only preached about the necessity of forgiveness; he practiced it to the extreme. He had every right to curse those who had abandoned him and those who had condemned him unjustly. Yet he does no such thing. He was perfectly consistent with his life lived as a free sacrifice of love so that even when all turned against him — " 'Crucify him' they all cried out" (Matt. 27:22) — he continued loving them. Nothing they could do would force him to stop loving them. He was hurt but not broken, disappointed but not discouraged, abandoned by all but abandoning no one. He had come to bring a new unity of love to humanity, and he would not allow the forces of ugliness, insult, torture, or even death to disrupt his mission. When all had broken with him, he broke with no one by forgiving everyone.

His very first words from the cross were a loving cry for forgiveness. God's love in and through Jesus was more powerful than all the evil forces that tried to destroy it. Even at the very moment Judas was betraying him with a kiss, he still called him friend (Matt. 26:50). Through loving forgiveness, people who had lived as enemies could now become friends, persons who had been rivals could now become collaborators, people who had been estranged from one another could now come together in harmony, people who had fought one another could now work together for peace. Those who were on fire for revenge could now forgive. This was the witness of the first Christians, for as Stephen was being stoned to death, he prayed for his murderers (Acts 7:54–60). This spirit of forgiveness continues through the early martyrs and even unto our day in the lives of people like the Maryknoll Sisters and the Oklahoma priest who were murdered in Central America. The Christian longs for forgiveness rather than revenge.

These new possibilities inaugurated by the loving sacrifice of Jesus were truly pleasing and satisfying to the Father who created us to live in creative harmony and lamented the crimes and atrocities of men and women who were destroying God's creation. Is there anything more pleasing and satisfying to a loving parent than to see the broken family come back together in peace, harmony, and joy? I am sure, in a very human way of speaking, that the Father was hurt to see the atrocities poured out upon his beloved son but at the same time very proud and happy that the Son did not give in but kept right on loving no matter what others said or did. This was the only way to truly rehabilitate humanity. Jesus was a true champion who through love triumphed over the demonic forces of evil. Jesus did not lower himself to the standards of a sinful humanity but rather elevated humanity to the standards of divine love. The triumph of divine love is the glory of God. "Father, the hour has come. Give glory to your son, so that your son may glorify you" (John 17:1). Divine love is the normal way of a redeemed humanity. This is truly the glory of God. As Jesus said to Martha: "Did I not tell you that if you believe you will see the glory of God" (John 11:40).

After the resurrection when Jesus makes his way back to visit with the very disciples who had abandoned him to offer them peace and reconciliation, he does not tell them to just forget the whole thing and act as if nothing had happened. He showed them his pierced hands and side (John 20:19–20). The pain was still there, and it would always be there, but he had risen above it. Some scars will never disappear, but we do not have to let them destroy us. We rise above the hurts of life not by ignoring them but by naming them and forgiving, for it is through forgiveness that dealing and new life come about.

But Jesus went even further than just forgiving, as if forgiving were not enough. At the final moments of his earthly life on the cross, Jesus was still reaching out to us and inviting us into a new unity by offering us an incredibly precious gift — the gift of his own mother. Nothing unites a family more than a loving mother. He told the disciple, and through him addressed every disciple: " 'Behold your mother' and from that hour onward the disciple took her into his care" (John 19:27). It is no wonder that Mary has played such a powerful and comforting role in the lives of Christians throughout the ages. She stood by the cross, and she stands by each one of us today. Jesus not only forgives but even in the midst of the excruciating pain gives us the most beautiful gift possible — a loving mother to keep the household together. Although theologies about Mary have certainly varied, the faithful have always intuited in Mary the acceptance and compassion of a loving mother.

There are many beautiful medieval stories about the compassion of Mary. One of my favorites is about Peter's complaint. When Jesus asked Peter why so many shady characters were getting into heaven, Peter complained that it was not his fault. An elderly lady, who happened to be Mary, was going around digging holes beneath the walls of heaven and sneaking in those who had been kept out. The more that preachers emphasized the horrors of purgatory and hell, the more the faithful told stories about the compassion of Mary.

Several years ago I attended a lecture on liberation given by an African American religious leader. He stressed that we could more easily be liberated from harsh laws and enslavement than from the inner enslavement of the spirit that still carries the ugly scars of slavery and humiliation deep within the soul. He went on to stress that true liberation would come only through forgiveness, and only when black people were free enough to offer a gift to those who had formerly enslaved them would they finally be free enough to say, "I'm a human being!" Only by the offering of the gift would the scars be healed and the freedom of the spirit be experienced. This is exactly what Jesus did from the cross: he forgave and offered us a gift.

No one has a right to speak evil about others, to curse others, to gossip maliciously, or to destroy another's reputation. No one has a right to exploit and even enslave the weak and defenseless. No one has a right to enjoy the misery and misfortune of others. No offense deserves forgiveness nor can forgiveness be demanded. Legal systems will demand punishment and retribution while the Christian spirit will go beyond the legal systems to offer forgiveness and reconciliation. Forgiveness comes through a love that is greater than the offense.

Forgiveness is not a form of weakness in those who are too cowardly to demand payment and justification. It is quite the opposite. It is not weakness but strength, a strength that comes through the life of God alive in us. I forgive not because I wasn't hurt, not because I am not in pain, not because I was not disappointed, not because now I approve of the evil action, not because I am too much of a coward to seek revenge. I forgive because my love is greater than the pain. I forgive because I do not want to contribute to the continuation of destructive violence. I forgive because God forgives, because

God has forgiven me and entrusted me with the ministry of reconciliation: "And all this is from God, who has reconciled us to himself through Christ and given us the ministry of reconciliation" (2 Cor. 5:18).

Nobody can hurt me more than the persons I love the most. The greater the love, the deeper the pain and the more difficult it is to forgive. But God is with us assuring us that God's grace is sufficient. Forgiveness will not be spontaneous and easy, no matter how holy we are, but it is possible and it begins with the recognition of how difficult it is and even seemingly impossible. It begins in the profound prayer that opens us to the power of the Spirit within us, as we admit our powerlessness and ask for God's help. It is the welcoming of the Spirit that enables us to cry out, "Abba, Father" (Rom. 8:15–16). The Spirit will guide us through any and all difficulties unto the path of true righteousness. Gradually, without even realizing it, the Spirit of love will lead us to forgive even while remembering the hurts.

An elderly lady, who happened to be Mary, was going around digging holes beneath the walls of heaven and sneaking in those who had been kept out.

At the end of life, there is nothing more peace-giving than to know that regardless of my faults, mistakes, and inadequacies God forgives me and takes me lovingly into God's loving heart. But there is a catch to this. Even though God's offer of forgiveness is there, I will not welcome it into my life unless I too have forgiven those who have offended me. In the forgiveness of others, I experience God's own forgiveness of me and can truly say, with Jesus: "Father, into your hands I commend my spirit" (Luke 23:46). I can then peacefully enter into the fullness of life with God and the entire communion of saints who have preceded me into eternal life. At that moment, the One who began the good work in us will bring it to completion (Phil. 1:6) and we will see God face to face and enjoy forever the banquet that awaits us.

> In him we have redemption by his blood, the forgiveness of transgressions, in accord with the riches of his grace that he lavished upon us. (Eph. 1:7–8)

> For in him all the fullness was pleased to dwell, and through him to reconcile all things for him, making peace by the blood of his cross (through him), whether those on earth or those in heaven. (Col. 1:19–20)

Sacraments of Baptism and Reconciliation: God's Offer of Rehabilitating Forgiveness

In the sacrament of Baptism our sins are forgiven, and we receive the gift of the Holy Spirit (Acts 2:38), empowering us to forgive as we have been forgiven. Yet Christ knew that this was only the beginning and that during our life we would fall again. Hence he gave the church the sacrament of Reconciliation. Through this sacrament we are given the opportunity to recognize our faults, repent and receive God's mercy. It is a beautiful opportunity to examine ourselves and cleanse ourselves so that we might continue on the road to final conversion at the end of our lives. It is a marvelous affirmation and healing to know that I have been forgiven by God and that I can truly "go in peace." I have seen people crying with joy at the realization that they are forgiven when they hear the words: "Go in peace, your sins are forgiven."

Greater Than Nuclear Energy

T HE WORLD OF TODAY, and especially our youth, feels intoxicated with the new wine of the atomic force. They exult in the thought that in their hands they have an almost unlimited source of energy. We have therefore a reason, my dear brothers, to say that today more than ever before we need the heart of Jesus to remain with us or return to our world. And the reason is precisely this: we live in the atomic age. It is as though an insane brat had got hold of a loaded pistol. Journalists have tried to give prominence these days to a period of my life when Providence willed that I should find myself in the zone blasted by the atomic bomb of Hiroshima and that I should escape unhurt. Well then, I remember that when I was still under the terrible impression of the catastrophe, in a conversation with some young students we were commenting on the power of the weapon employed and calculated the thousands of casualties in our neighborhood and those which might be expected as a consequence. I remember how, after a pessimistic diagnosis by the youths, a spontaneous observation occurred to me that impressed them profoundly: "And after all, my dear friends, in spite of this new powerful weapon and any others that may still come, you must know that we have a power much greater than atomic energy: we have the Heart of Christ. While atomic energy is destined to destroy and atomize everything, in the Heart of Christ we have an invincible weapon whose power will destroy every evil and unite the minds and hearts of the whole of mankind in one central bond, his love and the love of the Father."

— Pedro Arrupe, *In Him Alone Is Our Hope: Texts on the Heart of Christ (1965–1983)* (St. Louis: Institute of Jesuit Sources, 1984), 114–15

"Truly a spirituality for the 21st century!"
— *Dolores Leckey*

Catholic Spirituality for Adults

General Editor
Michael Leach

Forthcoming volumes include:

- *Listening to God's Word* by Alice Camille
- *Community* by Adela Gonzalez
- *Incarnation* by John Shea
- And many others.

To learn more about forthcoming titles in the series, go to *orbisbooks.com*.

For free study guides and discussion ideas on this book, go to *www.rclbenziger.com*.

Please support your local bookstore.

Thank you for reading *Charity* by Virgil Elizondo. We hope you found it beneficial.